Wild Daisies in the Sand

Wild Daisies in the Sand

Tom Sando
with J.P. Desgagne

NeWest
PRESS

National Library of Canada Cataloguing in Publication Data
Sando, Tom, 1922-
Wild daisies in the sand

Includes some text in Japanese.
ISBN 1-896300-51-0

1. Sando, Tom, 1922—Diaries.
2. Japanese Canadians—Evacuation and relocation, 1942-1945—Personal narratives.
3. World War, 1939-1945—Concentration camps—Ontario, Northern.
I. Title.
D805.C3S26 2002   940.53'177131'092   C2002-910991-4

Editor for the Press: Satya Das
Cover and interior design: Ruth Linka
Cover image: "Daisy and barbed wire on green background"
(Acrylic on board, 6" x 9") by Mike Reichert Steinhauer
Author photo: Everett Williams

Canadian   Patrimoine
Heritage   canadien

NeWest Press acknowledges the support of the Canada Council for the Arts, the Alberta Foundation for the Arts, and the Edmonton Arts Council for our publishing program. We also acknowledge the financial support of the Government of Canada through the Book Publishing Industry Development Program (BPIDP) for our publishing activities.

NeWest Press
201-8540-109 Street
Edmonton, Alberta T6G 1E6
(780) 432-9427
www.newestpress.com

02 03 04 05 4 3 2 1

PRINTED AND BOUND IN CANADA

TABLE OF CONTENTS

PREFACE

On the chilly morning of Saturday, December 6, 1941, my father, my younger brother Shig and I, Tamio Kuwabara aged nineteen, travelled across the choppy waters of the Georgia Strait on our small fishing boat *Hokui No. 1*. We tied our boat down in Steveston Harbour, on a pier belonging to the BC Packer Co., and began unloading our few household possessions.

Having made substantial profits from bountiful fishing trips catching shark and cod off the coast of Vancouver Island, we decided to rent a house in Steveston, British Columbia, just at the mouth of the Fraser River. This would be our place for the winter months. It was an exciting idea. Steveston was very near to my favourite city, Vancouver, and, compared to the isolated village of Skeena River in northern BC where I had spent the past four years fishing salmon, very close to civilization. We had a bright outlook and big plans. We were going to buy a larger boat next spring that would permit us to fish all year round. Of course we would be spending the salmon season, the months of July and August, in Skeena River, but we would return to fish the BC coast for halibut, cod and shark for the remainder of the year.

We expected a very prosperous year ahead of us, as the price of fish was soaring on account of the war in Europe. After the fishing experience my brother and I had gained over the past years, we would be capable of catching plenty more fish. Someday we would buy a beautiful house near Vancouver—our own house. I might even have the chance to go to school and learn some English in the off-season. Indeed, our future looked very promising.

Our bright future was shattered the following morning when we heard the shocking news on the radio—Japanese planes had bombed Pearl Harbour. The US and Canada immediately declared war on Japan. December 7, 1941 was a fatal day for Japanese Canadians, especially those living on the coast of British Columbia. The totality of the news stunned the entire Japanese community into shocked disbelief.

Ten days later we received a notice from the Royal Canadian Mounted Police to remove our fishing boat to an impound yard near New Westminster. We tied down our small fishing boat upstream on the Fraser River. It was heartbreaking to see our beloved boat left behind. I had no idea what would happen to our boat. It broke my heart to see my proud father weeping as we departed the cove where our boat was tied among hundreds of Japanese-owned boats. *Hokui No. 1* was an old boat, but my father had owned her for over sixteen years. He had loved his boat as if she was a dear wife. He promised us that some day he would come back to reclaim her. Unfortunately, that would never happen. Two years later he received a cheque for $250.00 from the Canadian government. They had sold his boat without consent. My brother Shig and I spent a quiet Christmas and New Year's together in a small rented house in Steveston, BC. Our Japanese neighbours shared our silent holiday spirit.

An uneasy feeling had begun to circulate within the Japanese community. Rumours were spreading that we would be chased out of the BC coast or even deported to Japan. All community Japanese schools had been shut down, and our short-wave radios had been taken from our homes. We were restricted from moving or travelling and we could go no farther than fifty miles without a permit. A curfew was imposed and all Japanese were forbidden to leave their homes after dark.

My brother and I made two or three trips out of Steveston to visit our father and stepmother in Vancouver. They were residing in a rooming house not too far from Powell Street. My stepmother was receiving treatment for her crippling rheumatism at a clinic in the city. My father stayed with her in Vancouver, and consequently my brother and I were left alone in Steveston. We made many friends our own age. We played table tennis, roller-skated and used the parallel bars to pass the time as there was no more fishing or other work to be done since the government had taken away our boats.

In early 1942, the Canadian government reinstated the War Measures Act, which enabled the Prime Minister to exercise a wide range of powers for the security, defence, order and welfare of Canada. Under this act, for "national defence and security reasons," Prime Minister Mackenzie King was empowered to restrict, evacuate, deport and detain any Japanese Canadian without ever imposing any formal charges.

Once these authorizations were handed down to the BC

Security Commissioner, the severe restrictions imposed on all Japanese Canadians inhabiting the West Coast region were immediately enforced. All persons of Japanese origin, regardless of citizenship, place of birth, or nationality, were regarded as potential enemy aliens. Our fishing boats, motor vehicles, radios, firearms and cameras were all confiscated.

Japanese families in the communities of British Columbia were handed a notice by the RCMP to appear for fingerprinting and photographing. Japanese Canadians were required to carry their registration cards with them at all times.

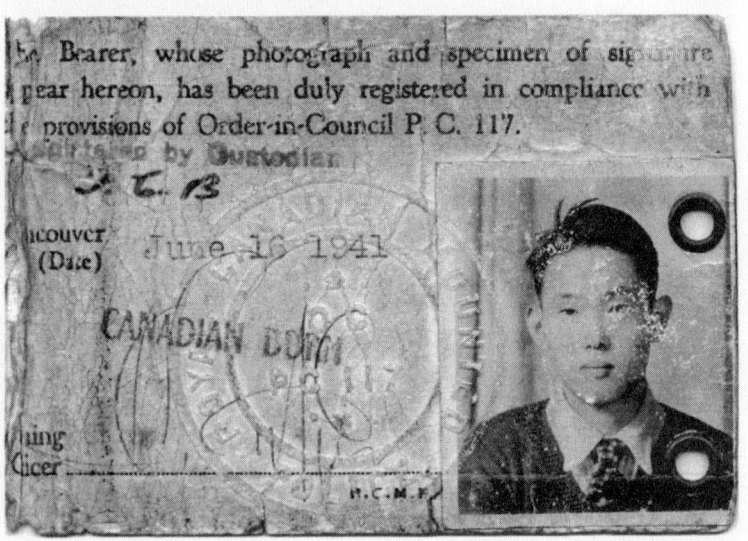

Suddenly, in early March 1942, all Japanese Canadians living on Vancouver Island and coastal regions (except Vancouver City and the nearby lower mainland) were removed from their homes. With only a few small personal possessions, entire families were herded into a temporary internment camp set up within Hastings Park, Vancouver. Soon thereafter began an evacuation of the twenty-one thousand Japanese Canadians from the "Defence Zone," an approximately one hundred-mile-wide coastal area of British Columbia. They were all destined to be evacuated to the relocation centres located somewhere in the interior of BC.

One by one, every able-bodied, single and married man between eighteen and forty-five was forcefully separated from his family and removed to road camps located within the interior of BC and Ontario. They were given no choice but to obey the orders. They were mercilessly compelled to leave their loved ones, wives, children, younger brothers and sisters, and aged parents behind. Those men who disobeyed were immediately detained by the RCMP and, very much like criminals, sent to concentration camps in remote areas of Eastern Canada. By the end of March, several of my friends had already been taken away from their homes and sent to the road-camps. With an uneasy feeling of apprehension, my brother and I sombrely awaited for our turn to be sent away to the road camps.

We were in complete turmoil. Everything we owned had been ruthlessly taken away from us. Worst of all, we were being separated from our beloved families. It was a painful time for us Japanese Canadians. I awoke one morning to discover that the white Canadians who had resented us for so long were now able to carry out their discrimination, with complete impunity. It was a time of utter loss for our people. Before this we lived peaceful lives in Canada, as respectable Canadian citizens. In all this time we had certainly done nothing to merit such brutality from the people of Canada.

I was a young Canadian and felt loyal to my country. I looked upon my Canadian flag with pride. It was good that I had been born in the greatest democratic country in the world. All of my life I had felt blessed with great honour and dignity. Now, in a very short time, I had been left bewildered, wondering where I really was and what had happened to my land of freedom. This is my story, as it happened when I was much younger, many years ago.

HASTINGS PARK

April 22, 1942

Six days ago, my brother and I received a notice from the RCMP to report to the BC Security Commission's office on April 22. On this day we were to be given train tickets that would take us to the road camp in an isolated region of the interior of British Columbia. Our parents had asked us to come and visit them for a few days prior to our departure. So we packed some belongings into suitcases and cloth bags, and moved out of our house in Steveston so that we could spend what little time remained with our parents in Vancouver. Today, our time of freedom was coming to an end. We are to be sent to an unknown road camp, possibly as early as tonight or the following morning.

The BC Security Commission's office is in Hastings Park, located on the east side of the city, at the very end of the streetcar line. The BC Security Commission handles the Japanese Canadians' registrations, custody of their properties (land, house, car, boat, furniture), and their relocations. Before the war, Hastings Park was a city-owned year-round recreational park with a big roller coaster and several entertaining horse tracks. The park had been hastily converted into a temporary internment camp for the Japanese Canadians, now forcibly evacuated from their homes on the West Coast.

At 10:00 AM, we got off the streetcar near Hastings Park and obtained an entrance permit from the guardhouse located at the gate. Everywhere I looked, the park was crowded with people. Men, women, young and old, (nearly three thousand) Japanese Canadians had arrived from various parts of the Pacific coast. They inhabited rebuilt shelters that had once been barns and stables for the park's racing horses.

Once inside the park I could hear all around me the sounds of carpenters' hammers and the laughter of children. It was a beautiful spring day; the cherry trees released a sweet fragrance in the air as they blossomed everywhere in the park. It was understandable that everyone felt they should be out in the fields enjoying the warm spring sunshine. It was an unusually strong sun for April, and it was far better to stay outside than be cooped-up in those filthy makeshift stables.

This was my first visit to the park since the war had begun. My father accompanied us, for he knew his way around. He had visited Hastings Park on several occasions to meet with his old friends from Skeena River who had earlier been interned. He led us straight to the Commissioner's office. Inside we found the place packed with waiting men, all wearing worried frowns on their tired faces.

Like myself, most of the men in the Commissioner's office were waiting for their papers to be sent to the government-appointed road camps. They were more concerned for the safety of their families than for themselves. I could see the loss that they felt, unable to protect their families and powerless to show their anger at being forced to leave them behind. Most of the men had submitted quietly, bowing in obedience to the government's orders. As the Japanese say, "*Shikata ga nai*," "It cannot be helped." However, my curiosity was aroused when I heard that there were some men protesting against the injustices of the Canadian government, and they were refusing to be removed.

After a long time, my name was finally called. I walked to the young Nisei clerk sitting behind the desk and gave him my papers. I was sent to a room next door for a physical examination.

My father had accompanied us to the Commissioner's office in hopes of negotiating the custody of our property and to arrange for the welfare of our ailing mother. He was told that the man in charge was Mr. Brown, and that he would not be in until the afternoon. So we decided to have lunch together while we waited. An RCMP officer escorted a group of us to the dining hall located a couple blocks from the Commissioner's office. After lunch, the same officer led us back to the office.

My brother and I were told that there would be a one-day delay before our departure to the road camp. We were scheduled to leave the train station at 6:00 PM tomorrow night. We were happy to be granted one more day of freedom in Vancouver. All of our ordered mandates had been fulfilled and still we had plenty of time left until curfew, so we decided to visit our old friends, the Tani brothers. They had been relocated earlier from Skeena River.

By chance, as we were leaving the office, we bumped into a couple of young boys we had known from Skeena River. They recognized us right away. I asked them if they could help us find the Tani brothers. They happily accepted our invitation and we followed them across a sunny flower garden. I gazed with wonder at their young sunburned faces and was surprised that they had grown up so fast in the short time since I had last seen them.

When we had departed from our small village six months ago, they had been skimpy little boys, innocently playing around our fishing nets set aside to dry on the piers. Most of them had never seen an automobile, horse or cow until they had arrived in Vancouver. No roads had connected our neighbouring villages; the only transportation possible was by boat. I could only begin to imagine how unsettling the experience had been for these small children, to have been abruptly uprooted from their homes and thrown into a big city among thousands of strangers. It was no wonder they had grown up so fast, with their adult gestures and the urbane manner in which they spoke. We continued to walk, carefree under the sun, to find the Tani brothers and they excitedly talked about all of their recent experiences.

We arrived at the men's compound where several hundred Japanese men were being held for temporary internment. The women and children were housed in a separate building. Once inside, I was immediately struck by the strong smell of disinfectant. The building was filled beyond capacity with army-style bunk beds. Piles of cloth bags were thrown about, leaving us very little room to walk. Running along the tops of the bunks were blankets and clothes that the men had hung to create some privacy. We could not see behind the many makeshift curtains, and so eventually made our way towards the exit.

Just as we were leaving the building, we noticed Kazuo Tani coming our way. It was such a wonderful feeling to see my old friend again! The good-tempered and easygoing Kazuo-kun and his brother Yoshikazu-kun had been best friends to my brother Shig and me since well before the war. The four of us had become as close as true blood brothers. They had lost their mother when they were young, and been brought up by relatives in Japan. They had moved with us from Japan to Canada in 1938, and lived in a house in Skeena River with their father and stepmother. Just like my brother and me.

We had so much to talk about. So many things had happened in the time since we had last seen each other in Skeena River six months before. We spoke of all the unfairness we had endured in the last few months. It felt good to share my thoughts with someone I knew so well. We talked as we walked outside towards a large flat building. Kazuo mentioned that this was where the women and children were being held. It seemed to us very unsanitary as it had been a horse stable before the war. A guard sat on a chair near the entrance reading a magazine. No men could enter unless they held a valid permit.

We continued our walk by a hospital that had been set up for the treatment of minor ailments. Kuzuo explained that a school had been built somewhere in the park, but there were not enough teachers and insufficient school supplies. He showed us a few more places and we walked to the park gate, then parted. It was shortly after 6:00 PM by the time we returned to our parents' rooming house, right on time for our curfew.

April 23, 1942

Although I had really tried to prepare myself, I could not help but feel the pain and sorrow of leaving my aged parents behind. A forced family separation was the cruellest thing that could ever happen to anyone in our society. It gave me great pain and anger to see so many Japanese families separated, forced apart like hapless slaves.

I had had a conversation with my parents a few days earlier. My stepmother suggested that we move to one of the sugar-beet farms in Alberta or Manitoba so that we could at least remain together. I firmly rejected her idea. I could not bear the thought of my aged parents doing hard labour in such a harsh environment. I told them that my brother and I would be all right and suggested that they go to the Greenwood Relocation Centre in the BC Interior. Once there, they would at least be living in a more comfortable climate and not be forced to do hard labour.

Our family gathered at the table for our last meal together, quietly discussing a place to meet after the war. We agreed that the best place would be in Japan, since our future in Canada had been made so uncertain. Stepmother carefully wrapped a *sushi-bento* in a paper bag, and told us to eat it on the train. It was so hard to see my beloved parents standing at the door, waving goodbye, having to leave them behind and not knowing when we would see them again. I looked at them standing there together under the doorway and wondered if they would ever be safe again.

My brother and I walked down to Powell Street to have one last look at the Japanese town. For many years this place had been a community centre and meeting place for the Japanese people. The barricaded stores and empty streets made me angry. I thought how sad it was that we had endured a life of repressed discrimination among the Canadian majority, while wishing all along merely to be accepted as equals. We were now forced to walk away from all of our residential and business property that had taken so many years of toil and labour to build. All lost to those who called us inferior because of the colour of our skin. There seemed to be no justice for our people. (In less than a year, Powell Street would be occupied mostly by Chinese Canadians.) After a while we said our final goodbye to our beloved Japanese town and caught a streetcar heading for Hastings Park. I thought this might be my last streetcar ride for a long time.

It was around 3:00 PM when we entered the BC Security Commissioner's office in Hastings Park. The office was as crowded today as it had been yesterday. A tall blonde man, who had interviewed us before, picked up a stack of files on his desk and bluntly told us that we were being sent to a road camp near Cambie Siding, BC. The train would be leaving sometime tomorrow and we were to remain in the park over night. He wrote our names and registration numbers down on a piece of paper and an RCMP officer escorted us to a brick building a block away. He locked the door behind us. The room was approximately twenty-five by fifteen metres, dimly lit, and packed with bunk beds. A big guard at the front entrance kept a keen eye on everyone inside and checked everyone entering or leaving the building.

We were each given three blankets and told to find an

empty bed, which we found in the right corner of the building. We set our bags down. There were a few small windows three metres above the floor, which gave me an unpleasant feeling of being imprisoned. After asking the guard a few times, he reluctantly gave us permission to go outside for a couple of hours. We met up with the Tani brothers talking with some friends in the park, and went for supper together in the dining hall. There were more than fifty men lounging inside our building by the time we had returned at around 7:00 PM. They were of all different ages, from as young as my eighteen-year-old brother to as old as forty. Almost all of the men were to be sent to the road camps.

I got into a friendly conversation with a group of young men from Vancouver Island. They informed me that they were to be sent to the Cambie Siding road camp, but they had decided that since this was not in their favour, they were not going. They asked us to join their resistance movement and fight for our human rights. I spoke with my brother and after taking a deep breath, we nodded in approval and gladly accepted their proposal. It was inspiring to meet such brave young men who were willing to stand up for their rights. We sat comfortably together for a time discussing how and when we would tell the Commissioner of our refusal to depart. After a while we decided to delay our plans until the next day.

I thought I recognized the elderly man mopping the floors of the building. I walked over to him and was happy to discover that he was an old friend of my father's. A WWI veteran, he smiled when I told him of my intention to fight for justice and gave me many heartening words of encouragement. At around

11:00 PM, my good friend Kazuo Tani, who had just happened to be the night watchman for our building, came to visit me. We spoke at length together, as best friends do on a warm and romantic evening, until all too suddenly it was well past midnight. It was after one when my good friend departed.

April 24, 1942

I awoke at 7:30 AM feeling very hungry. Our group of men waited quietly until an RCMP officer finally arrived to take us to the mess hall for breakfast at 9:30 AM. We quickly finished our breakfast and the officer escorted us back to the building, locking the door behind us.

The RCMP had tightened their security and we were no longer allowed to leave the building. There was no doubt that we were now being treated like criminals. A man from the building had gone missing and had not been found for some time. We were all suspect, now.

We soon grew restless. At 10:00 AM we found a way to leave the building through the back door. The sun blinded me as I walked outside. It took a while for my eyes to adjust to the natural light. With a feeling of relief, I lay down on the warm grass and looked up at the big blue sky. Large fluffy clouds floated silently above me. Everything in my view was filled with the pleasant glow of the warm spring sun. I thought it might be a long time before I could enjoy the sunshine again.

As wonderful as my moment of freedom was, it only lasted a couple of hours before I was forced back into the dark building. Just before 3:00 PM, after we received our train tickets to Cambie Siding, the RCMP allowed us to go outside again. This gave our group of nineteen men enough time to walk to the Commissioner's office and announce our intentions. When we told Mr. Taft, the commissioner in charge, that we were refusing to go to camp, his face turned as red as a beet. His voice was choked for a moment and then he slowly said that if we refused to go, we would be very sorry. He tried to persuade us to change our minds, but we were convinced that enough was enough. We ignored him and went back to our room.

At 5:00 PM, two RCMP officers entered our building and arrested our resistance leaders, E. Yoshikuni-kun and Y. Yoshida-kun. We were told that they were being detained for questioning. We sat together for a while in tense silence. Four men decided it would be best if they surrendered themselves to the authorities, and so they quietly left our group.

The time came to board the train for the road camp. The RCMP escorted all the Japanese men who had submitted to the order. Once they had departed for the train station, our small group of thirteen men began feeling nervous about our rebellious stance. We were going against all of Canada. We looked at each other and declared, "*Ganbarun dazo!*" We would stick together no matter what and fight for our rights and freedom.

Two RCMP officers came in and rudely took away our train tickets and registration cards. They left us with angry words, saying, "You'll be sorry!" We asked them where the two men had been taken, but they gave us no other reply.

I was getting very nervous. I had refused to go to the road camp and disobeyed the government's orders. I had never disobeyed any authority before, let alone something so serious. I was afraid I might be charged as a traitor and thrown into prison. Once the RCMP left with our train tickets and registration cards, I calmed down a little, and felt more confident, like a person who is waiting for his sentence. "*Yari demo teppo demo mottekoi!*" "I am not afraid of them anymore." We all grinned when we heard the train whistle. Then someone yelled, "The train is leaving!" There was no turning back now.

They guarded us much more closely now. We must have seemed like real troublemakers to them. When the guard followed me to the washroom, I could not help but give him a bitter smile. They tried to punish us by not giving us any supper. But we did not care because we had our own *bento*, given to us by our families for the long train ride. We talked among ourselves in confidence, as though we had known each other all our lives.

Everyone stuffed their shirts and pockets with cigarettes, candies and other essentials from their packs, just in case we were to be removed suddenly in the night. We were uncertain but suspected that our resistance would land us all in prison. It did not matter, for then at least we would know where we stood. After waiting anxiously until it was apparent that nobody was coming for us, we finally went to bed.

THE IMMIGRATION BUILDING

April 25, 1942

I awoke feeling refreshed. Yesterday had been a very exciting and troubled day, yet I still managed to get a good sleep. An RCMP officer led our group of detained Japanese men to the mess hall for breakfast at around 9 AM. We were escorted back to our compound as soon as we had finished our meal. We were given no idea what would become of us. As we silently contemplated our stand against authority, all of us seemed prepared for the worst.

An RCMP officer told us to get ready for transportation to the Immigration Building. At 10:00 AM an RCMP wagon pulled up to our building. Several RCMP pushed us into the small wagon and two officers jumped in behind us to guard the back door. After a half-hour drive across Vancouver, we arrived at the front steps of the Immigration Building. Two armed soldiers opened the back doors and we climbed out onto the pavement.

The RCMP handed over some papers to a waiting military guard and, after a few brief words, climbed back into the wagon and drove away. It came to me as a shock when I realized that the army was now involved. The guard looked at us and carefully folded the papers, then escorted us single file into the building.

I vividly remembered coming to this same building four years earlier. Back then I had eagerly presented my Canadian birth certificate to a customs officer and explained that my father had sent me to Japan when I was only four years old. I had lived there until the age of sixteen, when I decided to come back home to Canada to live with my father. It seemed like only yesterday that my heart was filled with such hopes and dreams for my country.

Today was a different day. I felt despondent. I was a prisoner in my own land because of the crime of my skin colour. Now that I had resisted the government's orders, I was sure to be punished.

Two guards searched us at the door and seized my pocketknife. Once they had completed their search, they gave us some blankets and led us to a large empty room. A big steel door locked us in. There were enough bunks inside to accommodate more than five times our number. A large dining and recreation area was connected to our room, directly to the north.

I looked through a small barred window facing to the east and saw a sidewalk three storeys below. It led to the Canadian Pacific Rail station and its many wooden platforms. I moved to a window on the north wall and saw a spectacular view of North Vancouver outlining the wooded area of Stanley Park. I watched as small boats sailed among larger freighters moving from the Vancouver harbour into the blue ocean waters beyond. The sight of this urban scenery relaxed me a little. I thought about the two group leaders who had been taken away earlier and had not been seen since. I was worried for my friends and wondered if I would ever see them again.

After lunch I spoke to our group about these missing men. No sooner had I begun to speak than they walked in through the door smiling, with blankets under their arms. We immediately surrounded them and cheered as though they were mighty heroes at a long-awaited homecoming.

We slowly began to settle down in our respective bunk beds. I was stirred by one of our fellows who was excitedly pointing out of the east window. We crowded around the small window to have a better look at what was happening down below. Several cars had arrived and were parked along the side of the street. A crowd of Japanese men were pressing against the entrance doors, demanding to be allowed entry into our building. One of the men below took notice of us at the window and shouted, "Don't worry, we'll be up in no time." It gave me comfort to see the crowd of men gathering in support of us. The guard at the doors left the crowd to get his superior. After an hour of much heated debate, the deputy of the Security Commissioner threw his hands up in the air and allowed them into the building. Our room soon became filled with the clamour of excited voices.

The Mass Evacuation Movement Group had only recently been formed, and was made up of mostly of young Nisei, Japanese men born in Canada. Their parents, wives, and children had already been taken from them and relocated in temporary settlements in the interior of British Columbia. There was still a large number of Japanese Canadians residing in

Hastings Park and the surrounding area of Vancouver. Men who were still awaiting their internment orders had organized a group to protest the Canadian government's unfair legislation of family separation. The group made a formal request that they be evacuated to the same location as their families so that they could live together. Their request was flatly rejected by the government. As a result, the group refused to be removed to the road camps. They had turned themselves over to the Immigration Building for voluntary detainment.

Our small group was the first to resist the government and it was encouraging to see other men follow in our protest. As the twilight descended across the auburn sky into our windows, the new group of men settled down in their bunk beds. I returned to my bunk near the north window and looked out of the barred window at the glimmering city lights below. Curled up atop my bunk, I felt like a stranger in a far away place.

April 26, 1942

We received one boiled egg and two slices of toast each for breakfast this Sunday morning. At around 10:00 AM, some of our friends and relatives came to visit us, but the guards forbade them entry to our building. We opened the east window so we could speak with them. They seemed happy to be able to share some talk with us while standing on the sidewalk below. They proudly showed us the generous supply of food they had brought us. *Sushi, manju,* and chocolates all made a tasty treat.

All day long, men crowded around the two small windows set at the east of our room, trying to see their visitors. Some of the men began to scuffle for a better place near the window. No

TOM SANDO

more than a minor commotion ever broke out, as we had a sound respect for each other. To the people looking up from down below, we must have looked like excited monkeys dangling in a cage.

Our visitors came steadily throughout the day, some coming from Vancouver and others from distant rural areas. I felt encouraged by their support, knowing that they were behind us all the way. I was proud that we Nisei had the will to fight for our rights. We were Japanese Canadian citizens and deserved our proper share of rights and freedom. As the day wore on, more and more it felt that we were doing the right thing. To sit back and say *"Shikata ga nai,"* that it could not be helped, now seemed like a total shame. Today we could make a show and stand for our rights.

Looking out of my window I observed the distant mountain range fading away into the misty twilight horizon. Another exciting day was almost over. Our visitors had departed, leaving before their appointed curfew.

April 27, 1942

All day long people visited us from the sidewalk below and delivered packages to be taken up by the guards. They brought us *nigiri-meshi* (rice balls), oranges, cigarettes, candy, books and towels. They also brought some news of a disturbance in Hastings Park resulting from a sudden food shortage.

I grew more acquainted with the men around me. It felt as though we had been together all of our lives. They came from all walks of life: fishermen, loggers, farmers, factory workers, shopkeepers, and students. Our conversations made the time go by quickly and sometimes, when we played cards, I almost forgot about my confinement. But looking at the visitors below through a barred window quickly brought me back to reality.

At 10:00 PM, a sergeant major accompanied by a guard inspected our room and departed after taking a roll call.

April 28, 1942

This afternoon, we were permitted to collect some items from our bags, which had arrived here in another vehicle. We descended to the second floor and collected our bags set on a table. I found my suitcase and took out a pen, notepad and some books.

Upstairs, a guard was sitting behind a steel door. Every time the guard heard the steel doors unlock, he opened his sleepy eyes and looked around to see who was coming. The gun at his side reminded me of the gravity of our situation. I grew disturbed by the echoing sound of that metallic door. It reminded me all too well of my unfortunate situation.

April 30, 1942

My sixth day of confinement within the Immigration Building. There were visitors at the front of the building all day long. The sun-filled window was constantly crowded with men talking with their friends and relatives down below.

From our dining room window, I could see the Vancouver harbour lying still in the morning air. It lifted my spirits a little to look at the large open scenery. A fishing boat with small red flags and buoys tied to its sides glided across the mirror-still waters of Burrard Inlet. In more peaceful times, at this time of year I would be fishing for halibut. With my father steering the boat, my brother Shig and I would cast our lines and let them fall to the ocean bottom. We would fish the open waters near the Queen Charlotte Islands from daybreak well into the afternoon. I always preferred fishing halibut to salmon. To be carried gently by the swaying waves so far away from the bustle and noise of civilization, in cheerful tranquillity, together with my brother and father, alone at sea. I had no idea what had become of our family fishing boat. The last time I had seen *Hokui No. 1* was along the Fraser river in New Westminster, where it was tied down among hundreds of impounded Japanese boats. A painful anger filled me as the fishing boat drifted away beyond my sight.

Our thin wool blankets did little to keep us warm at night. A few of the men were coming down with colds. The food was getting worse. For breakfast we each had one boiled egg and two slices of toast. For lunch they served us heaping clumps of macaroni and for supper a small helping of rice-curry stew. I should not expect any luxuries in here; after all, I had come here of my own free will.

One thing we were blessed with was the sergeant major in charge of the guards. He was an amiable young man who listened and really seemed to care. He was strict when it came to making our beds. Some days he would come in and arm-wrestle with some of the men. He sometimes played a little ping-pong and some of the men even began teaching him *Shogi*, Japanese chess. I respected his authority and grew to enjoy his company.

May 2, 1942

A light rain continued outside until noon. I could faintly see the mountain peaks of North Vancouver rising through the low-hanging clouds. The silk-like rain soaked the streets below and left a sheen on the parked cars. I heard a lazy whistle from an incoming ship far out of port.

In the afternoon we became excited by a rumour that we would be transferred the next day to a camp somewhere in Ontario. But later the sergeant major clarified that he would be the one transferred tomorrow.

We each contributed twenty-five cents as a farewell gift, to show our appreciation for his goodwill towards us. He was quite surprised when he came in to say goodbye. His face lit up with a pleasant glow of gratitude.

May 3, 1942

Today being Sunday, and the weather nice, more people came to visit us under our small windows. All day long, men crowded the windows, and when they saw a young woman in the crowd below, raised a shout of lively excitement. A few of the men were even given permission to go downstairs to the entry-way to see their visitors.

There was a change of guards this afternoon. The old guard-shift boarded an army truck and drove away. A couple of them waved goodbye to us.

May 5, 1942

It seemed like the weather would be spring-like today. The distant urban scenery could be seen vaguely through the light morning mist. The sun lifted across the sky and the mist vanished, leaving the city streets bustling with people bound for their destinations.

Men lingered by the windows, their eyes watching the outlying streets, always hopeful that they would spot some Japanese people coming their way. All of a sudden, I heard, "Hey, some Japanese women are coming our way!" All of us dashed for the open window. We let out a loud sigh as they turned the corner just out of our sight, a block away.

The activity around our windows continued with steady devotion all day. Everyone was anxious to see the visitors, regardless of who they had come to see. It became our greatest pastime.

R. Yoshida-san, a good friend of my father from Vancouver, came to visit us in the late afternoon. We had been restricted to speaking in English only, but today we spoke in Japanese, regardless. He informed us that our parents had already been moved to a settlement near Greenwood, British Columbia. He mentioned they were living in an abandoned mining town, hastily reconstructed to accommodate the large number of evacuated women, children, and elderly Japanese Canadians. Greenwood, Grand Forks, Lemon Creek, New Denver, Roseberry, Sandon, and Kaslo were all reconstructed ghost towns. I was relieved to know that my parents were together.

May 7, 1942
Our situation changed dramatically today. The guards entered our room and for no apparent reason forbid us to talk to our visitors. After a while, they started chasing our visitors away at

gunpoint. The men at the window grew furious when they realized what was happening. The brutality of our visitors being chased away at gunpoint was too unsettling for the men. They grabbed the window bars and shouted fiercely at the guards. A husky, *judo nidan*, black belt, pressed his head against the bars and started singing at the top of his lungs *"Aikoku koshin kyoku"* and soon all of us were crowded around the window singing "We love our country."

Pedestrians began to gather around the building as the singing continued well past sundown. All the tension of the past weeks had finally collapsed our civility. Locked together in this desperate time, we sang at the top of our lungs to quiet the noise of our situation. By the end of the day we could only speak in hoarse whispers.

May 8, 1942

Our room was becoming overcrowded. Some twelve more men joined us this morning. The guards opened a spare room at the rear of the building to accommodate them.

Perhaps as a result of our vocal protest yesterday, our visitors were allowed to come back. Some of us were even permitted to go downstairs and see them.

We collected about one hundred dollars between us and contributed it to the Mass Evacuation Movement Group in support of its efforts.

May 9, 1942

Two men who arrived here yesterday shared a disturbing story with me. They have been living in a road camp near Banff for the past few weeks. The camp is comprised of tents set at the base of a damp mountainside. Their living conditions are made extremely miserable by the wet and cold climate. On top of it all is the looming threat of an avalanche from the melting snow on the mountain.

Last week, a few men from their crew were injured by falling rocks. The two men here today are no longer interested in risking their lives by working in such dangerous conditions. Their refusal to work led the RCMP to arrest them and bring them here. If their story is true, I am glad that I did not go to any road camp.

Visitors informed us that the internment of Japanese Canadian families in the interior of British Columbia is in full scale. Some families have chosen to work in the sugar-beet plantations of Alberta and Manitoba so they could remain together.

We had a roast beef dinner, which came as a surprise from the every day macaroni and stew. As we ate, we were entertained by Mori-kun's outrageously funny war stories. We have nicknamed him Joto-hei (sergeant), as he was a sergeant in the ongoing war between Japan and China.

May 11, 1942

There was a light rain again this morning. I noticed the grass on the embankment near the waterfront is growing longer and the leaves on the poplar trees are becoming greener. Ships continually sound their arrival and departure from the nearby harbour.

The sky cleared up nicely by the afternoon. We received a group of visitors from Camberland, Vancouver Island. Most of the men were given a chance to go downstairs to meet with their visitors.

Later in the afternoon, we heard a disturbance on the street below. Some twenty or more Japanese Nisei were trying to enter the building. The guards refused to let them in so they all sat down near the entrance and started eating their *bento* lunches. The guards became furious and tried to chase them away at gunpoint, but they only lifted their heads and continued silently eating their lunches. We watched them nervously from our windows as the time approached curfew.

The guards finally realized that there was no way to chase the group away and so decided to allow them into the building. We heard some loud war cries as they approached our room. The guards led them into a small room adjacent to ours. There was a wall that separated us but we were able to communicate through small windows connecting the two rooms.

May 12, 1942

The guards' attitudes were much different towards us this morning, probably on account of yesterday's commotion. They informed our visitors that from now on only women are allowed to visit, and that we must communicate in English only. I felt sorry for an elderly man who left the sidewalk, sadly dispirited, now unable to speak with his son at the window.

At around 10:00 AM, the situation grew worse when the guards changed their minds and started chasing our visitors away. An elderly woman refused to leave until she could speak to her son. The guards drew their pistols and mercilessly forced her away. They chased our visitors for three blocks before finally turning back. I could see our visitors huddled together by an overpass, waving their handkerchiefs. We found our handkerchiefs and waved back. Some of us began shouting at them to come back, but they were already too far away.

We sent our spokesman Hayashi-san to appeal to the head guard but it was to no avail.

May 13, 1942

We sent a letter to the Security Commissioner after breakfast, requesting his audience with regards to yesterday's upsetting incident. A guard came back shortly after with a message that the commissioner had agreed to meet with us at ten this morning.

At 10:00 AM, the same guard came back and told us to wait until noon. We waited until 1:00 PM and began to feel like they were really not taking us seriously. So we wrote them an ultimatum, stating that if an official did not meet with us by 2:00 PM this afternoon, we would not be held responsible for any drastic event that may occur.

We waited anxiously, watching as the hands on the clock slowly passed the appointed hour of 2:00 PM. The sharp crashing sound of breaking glass suddenly broke our tense silence. I turned to see that one of the men had thrown a chair through the dining room window. This seemed to be our signal and all seventy of us initiated a fanfare of mayhem and destruction. The tension that we had endured for the past weeks had boiled over.

The room was filled with the deafening sounds of angry screams and breaking furniture. A frightened guard came to the steel door and pleaded with us to stop so that he could at least talk it over with his superior. We quieted enough to hear his pleas and agreed to stop for the moment. We were still breathing hard when the guard came back and asked for our spokesman to come downstairs to negotiate our situation. We told him no. We were not willing to take the chance that he would be arrested and told him that we all wanted to negotiate with the commissioner. He replied that this was impossible and left. Our anger was immediately rekindled and we began our destructive frenzy anew.

This time, we broke all four dining room windows and threw the folding tables against the walls. Metal bars and glass shards crashed onto the pavement down below as men smashed the window frames.

A crowd of civilians had begun to gather on the Canadian Pacific Rail overpass, behind the barricades that the guards had set up. We spotted some of our visitors and waved our hand-kerchiefs while shouting "Don't worry!" and singing "*Aikoku koshin kyoku*" at the top of our lungs. Some people from the neighbouring twenty-two storey Marine Building began looking down from their windows. Someone threw a roll of toilet paper that unfurled as it descended to the ground.

We rammed a steel bunk bed into a wall and after repeated attempts made a large jagged opening into the adjacent room. Men started dismantling the beds and throwing metal crossbars into the walls. Broken debris was scattered everywhere. Smashed doors and broken walls made the room resemble the aftermath of a violent earthquake.

At around 5:00 PM, a guard approached our door and timidly proposed that we talk things over. By this time, most of us had settled down and resorted to banging on the walls. Our representative, Hayashi-san, went to meet with him at the door. We calmed down then and the guard said that Hayashi-san could come downstairs, but we flatly refused. It was not too long before we resumed our steady banging.

Eight army trucks pulled up and eighty to ninety soldiers rushed out and quickly surrounded the building. I stuck my head out of the window to observe their exaggerated manoeuvres and heard several gunshots being fired. A bullet whistled past my ear and struck the bathroom wall behind me. A sudden fear clutched my insides and I threw myself to the floor. Never in my life had I been shot at. It scared the hell out of me.

Several canisters were fired into the open windows and a nauseous-smelling yellow smoke began to fill the room. The gas quickly spread into the adjacent rooms. My eyes and face burned terribly, bringing tears to my eyes and making them burn even more. A man next to me shouted "*Chikisho!*" Bastards! Someone in the room said to quickly cover our faces with wet towels. We dashed to the washroom and I placed a wet towel over my face. Almost overcome with pain, we began crawling madly to find any small area that might shelter us from the painful fumes.

To our relief, a breeze coming through the open windows took with it the foul vapours. We exulted in the clean air. The event left us broken, with little desire left for revolt. It took more than three hours for the gas to entirely dissipate from our rooms. As the sun began to set, a guard approached the men in the adjacent room. They had been much quieter than us and were asked to go outside and clean up the debris outside the building. They refused. The guards threatened that no supper would be brought until someone cleaned up the pavement. No one replied.

Our room had grown very timid. We satisfied our hunger with our remaining supply of candy and lay still on our scattered mattresses, exhausted by the day's events. I could see the city lights from where I sat. They appeared clearer now that the bars and glass were gone, suggesting that all was peaceful and nothing bad had ever happened. I could sense the presence of the soldiers outside and knew that things had gone badly. I dared not go to the window for a better look.

May 14, 1942

In spite of my empty stomach, I had a good sleep last night. I stayed in bed until 10:00 AM, thinking how it was lucky that none of us was injured during yesterday's calamities.

We have not received any food for almost twenty-four hours. This is the first time in my life that I have gone without food for so long. I do not understand how anyone could ever fast for so long. Voluntarily going without food for any period of time is incomprehensible to me. My hunger had bothered me the most last night, before bed. My food craving subsided and as the day wore on I was left feeling weak and tired.

All Japanese visitors are forbidden to approach the Immigration Building. The guards turn them back at the CPR station and at Pender Street. The soldiers still patrol the area with a noticeable display of authority. At 7:00 PM a Chinese waiter dressed in a sparkling white suit brought us some food. Two guards watched us as we silently ate our supper.

May 15, 1942

We had breakfast at 7 AM as usual. A guard asked us to send ten men downstairs to clean the debris around the building. After a short meeting we agreed to send some men down.

I was expecting some form of retribution or punishment for our destructive revolt, but nothing was ever brought up by the guards or anyone else. Maybe it was that they believed the incident could have been avoided had they simply granted us a brief meeting with the British Columbia Security Commissioner.

TO EASTERN CANADA BY TRAIN

May 16, 1942

It looks to be another fine day outside. A guard came up at noon and told us to get ready for our departure. We are being moved to a camp somewhere in Ontario. Everyone cheered. We have all been waiting for this order with great anticipation. At long last the day has come for our relief from this dreary building. I inhaled a breath of cool, fresh air near my window and smiled, looking out towards the distant mountains of North Vancouver.

At around 6:00 PM we filed downstairs and were soon all outside, observing the brick building that has held us captive for the past twenty-three days. Being outdoors felt good. The men around me were talking with a renewed spirit, as though reborn from the outside air. I observed the two small broken windows where we had spent so much time. I could now imagine what we looked like to our visitors, with our faces packed in those tiny openings.

Soldiers flanked our sides and we were marched to the CPR station. When we first arrived at the Immigration Building, we were only thirteen men. Now we are 136 men, all willing and ready to board a train. I settled into one of the three coaches.

道目指すは何處　如何ならん。暗澹たる前途を切開

き光明を齎らさんと動亂の眞たゞ中に飛び込んだ血氣

盛りの硬骨漢百五名第一世第二世の先發隊の勇士

越えて行くは幾山河幾千里　旅情又一入魂を打つて我が

東行譜は永く胸に高鳴り續けるであらう。

As the slow-moving train passed through Vancouver, we spotted some Japanese people standing by the railroad embankments, tearfully waving us goodbye. The train began to gain speed once it passed the city centre and crossed into the Burrard Inlet. The urban landscape faded behind me, leaving an empty feeling of longing in my heart. I bid a silent farewell to the city I had loved so much.

The coach I am in is probably the oldest coach they could find. The stiff seats and dust in the air make it very stuffy and uncomfortable. All the double-glassed windows are locked shut. Two armed guards watch us closely from the front and rear of the coach.

The sky began to darken and large food trays were wheeled in from the front of the train. We were served canned salmon, cheese, and sardines, plenty of bread and butter, coffee, and juice. It was a great feast for us, after the paltry meals we had endured in the Immigration Building. We were all famished and ate like starved children, ravenously eating without any care or etiquette.

The train tracks below tap a gentle cadence as we travel on our journey towards the east. I feel relaxed. The good food has been plentiful and I am now comfortably exhausted. I feel the long days of my confinement slowly ebbing into a passing memory. I curl up beside my brother on the hard narrow seat and try to sleep, but the confined coach and my excited mind keep me awake for several hours.

May 17, 1942

I must have slept for hours. The sun was already rising when I awoke, my back was stiff and my legs were cramped. I stretched and felt the blood flow to my sleeping legs. The slow-moving train was labouring up a steep incline. I marvelled at the breathtaking scenery outside. To see such huge and rocky mountains so close was spectacular. I heard an excited cry from the other end of the coach. Everyone rushed to look out of the window. A herd of elk was standing in a small flower-covered field, casually looking up at our train.

All day long I enjoyed the magnificent view of the Rocky Mountain wilderness. We travelled right through the mountains. I saw crystal-blue streams falling into forbidden canyons that dropped hundreds of feet to invisible depths far below. I was amazed by the towering mountains, which were so far away but filled all of my sight. I noticed how each one was similar but uniquely different from the next.

Our little train arrived at the famous Banff resort in the early evening. We stopped at the station and were all ready to go outside and stretch our legs, when the guards stopped us. We waited as several guards left the train and entered the station. An hour passed before they came back. A whistle blew and we were soon moving at full speed again. By sundown the mountains had receded behind us and we descended into the flatlands of Alberta.

May 18, 1942

I slept well through the night and I awoke at 6:00 AM feeling refreshed. We had travelled across Alberta and were now on the vast plains of Saskatchewan. The endless green fields stretched as far as I could see. Occasionally, we passed by a few cows standing in muddy fields near isolated farmhouses. Most of us on the train had never seen this land before, having been born and raised on the Pacific Coast. Seeing the peaceful scenery pass by made it hard to believe that the world was now engulfed in an ugly war.

Later in the evening we arrived in Winnipeg. The train stopped briefly to allow Takahashi-san to be taken to the hospital. He had been shivering with a cold sweat since the time we left Vancouver. I prayed for his health.

We swiftly crossed the flat Prairie provinces and entered into Ontario. The scenery changed profoundly. We were now travelling beside a chain of tiny lakes that were densely surrounded by flourishing jack pines and spruce bushes. Under an auburn sky, our train continued on its steady journey east.

May 19, 1942

Our little train passed through Port Arthur at 6:00 AM. All day long we passed by the vast waters of Lake Superior. It looked like an endless sea, with myriad flowing ripples of white-capped waves washing up onto the sandy shores. I looked out and thought that we had finally arrived to Eastern Canada, a place I had never believed I would ever come to.

PETAWAWA CONCENTRATION CAMP

May 20, 1942

We were awoken in the early morning hours. The guards walked down the aisles and told us to wake up and get ready for disembarking. Not long thereafter, the train stopped in a deserted field beside a few old shacks and broken-down fences. For three days and four nights we had journeyed by train across Canada. It was a good feeling to get off the stuffy coach and stretch my legs. I inhaled deeply the morning air, so sweet compared to the stale air back in our coach.

As soon as we stepped off the train the guards directed us into some waiting army trucks. I noticed as we drove away that we were being escorted by two smaller vehicles carrying soldiers armed with sub-machine guns. It was evident that they regarded us as prisoners of war. I supposed they had no way of knowing that we were just a bunch of unfortunate Canadians unwilling to harm anyone.

We travelled on a dusty gravel road for forty minutes, until the surrounding forest opened into a vast clearing. The truck stopped and we filed out in front of a large wire gate set between two wooden watchtowers. A three-metre-high barbed wire fence encircled a busy military compound. Four ten-metre-high watchtowers stood ominously above it all. Inside were whitewashed buildings and men walking together in small groups. They were wearing denim uniforms with bright red stripes descending along the pants and caps, and a large red circle on the backs. They looked like clowns waiting for the circus to begin. E. Yoshikuni-kun turned to me and casually mentioned that the red patch would make a good target for the guards to shoot at.

Seeing the camp as a whole made my heart beat a little faster. I felt as though I had suddenly come to the end of my road. I truly believed that once inside the compound I would be condemned beyond the point of no return. Even though I had been confined behind bars in Hastings Park and at the Immigration Building, I had still maintained a small sense of freedom. Perhaps the knowledge that I was still in Vancouver had given me some added confidence. But as I looked at the menacing watchtowers, the jagged barbed wire fences, and the men in uniforms, I knew deep down that I was *toraware no mi;* very much a prisoner.

We were marched into the camp and led into a small wooden building. A guard told us to remove our clothes and place them on a table. We nervously waited for a while before a doctor came in and examined us. My wristwatch, notebooks, and money were confiscated. We were forbidden from carrying any currency inside the camp.

After our examination, we dressed and were led across a field to temporary quarters. Seven large canvas tents were lined up beside a barbed wire fence. Across the fence I could see an adjacent camp where men were playing ball. Someone mentioned that they were German and Italian prisoners of war.

Later in the afternoon we were sent to another building to claim our bags and suitcases. The army quartermaster gave us each a hat, sweater, jacket, suspenders, shoes, and two pairs of wool socks. We removed our clothes once more and changed into the prison uniforms. These garments were much too big for us and were never intended for small Japanese men. Some men were given size ten shoes, fully three sizes too big. Once we had dressed, we all looked like prisoners, as if we belonged in a prison camp. A new life had begun for me. I was now officially a prisoner and began to wonder how long I would be kept here.

I later discovered that this facility was being used as a POW camp. Prior to our arrival at Petwawa, there were 229 Japanese men who had been interned here since the beginning of the war. Many of these men were arrested and imprisoned on charges of suspicion of espionage. In actuality, these men were harmless Japanese language-school principals, newspaper editors, church ministers, and other leading members of Japanese communities. They had been arrested as dangerous enemies under the Canadian War Measures Act.

I was assigned to the number-five tent with my close friends the Yoshikuni brothers, Yoshida-san, the Okazaki brothers, my brother Shig and the original group of men I was with at the Immigration Building. The tent held ten sets of double-decker bunks that could accommodate twenty inmates. The temperature cooled very rapidly once the sun descended behind the treeline. It had been an exhausting train ride followed by an eventful day. I was very tired. I lay down on a top bunk and pulled the blankets over my head to hide from the buzzing mosquitoes.

May 21, 1942

It is a clear morning, not a cloud in the sky. The grass is still wet from the morning dew, the ground comfortably soft under my feet. A light breeze gently brushes my face, bringing with it the fresh scent of nearby green poplars. The leaves on the trees surrounding the camp are shimmering under the bright morning sun. I grasp the entire beauty of the place and am left with a good impression on my first morning here in this camp.

The barbed wire fence and watchtowers surround four sets of converted army barracks that are joined by washrooms at the centre. These are our barracks, or "huts." Three of the huts house the 229 internees and the fourth is used as a kitchen and dining room. Connecting the eastside of the camp is another compound with similar barracks. These accommodate several hundred German and Italian prisoners of war.

A dense coniferous forest encircles the barbed wire fence

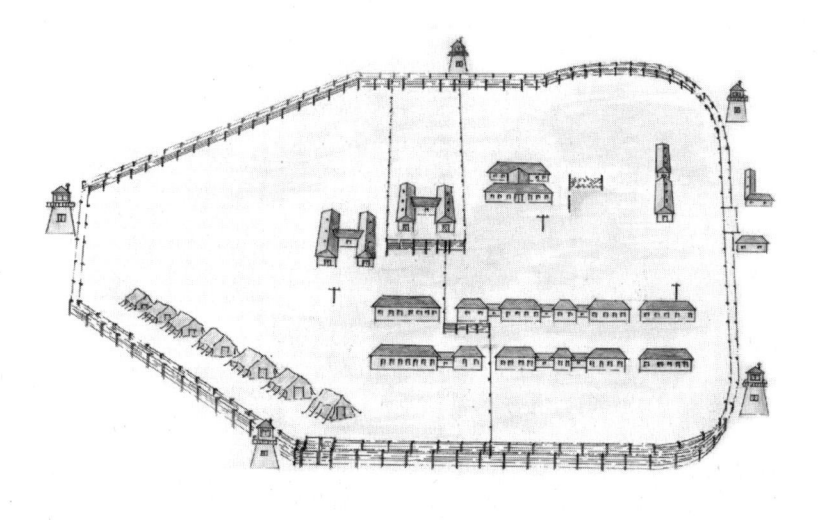

that in turn encloses our compound. The main gate is located to the south. There is a small opening in the treeline to the north. Beyond the opening is a dark-blue lake that serenely reflects the sky and surrounding trees upon its calm surface.

I wrote a letter to my father in the afternoon. I informed him that Shig and I are doing well and that we have been relocated to Petawawa. We are permitted to send three letters and four post cards a month. A guard gave us each an extra blanket, as some of the men were cold in their tents last night. The presiding camp leader informed us of our duties while we are in the camp. The kitchen and dining crews are voluntary, but we are all required to perform mandatory camp chores during the week.

After supper, the camp held a sumo-wrestling event as a welcoming gesture for us newly arrived internees. We lined up for the evening roll call at 9:00 PM, then were all sent to our respective tents and barracks for the night. It is nice and cool during the day, but it grows terribly cold at night. At 10:00 PM we were given a call for lights out. It was quiet for the first few minutes then tents three and four steadily became noisy. The sound of men talking and laughing continued late into the night.

May 22, 1942
I could hear rain drops falling gently on our tent early in the morning. At 6:00 AM a trumpet broke the silence. All around me, men began getting up. We assembled together and walked to the dining room for breakfast at 6:30. There was barely any water leakage in our tent this morning, but it grew considerably worse by the afternoon. Most of our bunks were completely

soaked by mid-afternoon. We were forced to move to a barracks for the time being.

May 24, 1942

Sunday today. We were allowed to sleep in until 7:00 AM. The rain stopped yesterday and we all moved back to our tents. I wrote a letter to my stepbrother Fukuji in Japan, informing him of my situation in Canada and asking for some war news from Japan. I have no idea if and when he will receive my letter.

May 25, 1942

We received a report from our camp commander stating that Takahashi-san has passed away. I thought it was really sad and felt that he was our first casualty of war. At 7:00 PM we held a memorial service in his honour. His two sons spoke a few quiet words to commemorate him.

May 27, 1942

Today was Japan's Navy Day. In 1904 Navy Admiral Togo vanquished the Russian fleet in the Sea of Japan. We gathered on the grounds facing the eastern sky and sang *"Kimiga Yo"* before the morning roll call. We held another sumo-wrestling event to celebrate the day. The event lasted all afternoon. Our cheering sounds were so loud that we attracted the neighbouring Germans and Italians, who gathered in crowds to watch behind the fence.

During the afternoon a high-ranking government official arrived from Ottawa to visit our camp. Our Nisei representatives went to see him but were turned away. He explained that the purpose of his visit was to speak only with the Issei, Japanese nationals. We Nisei were upset. Our representatives were going to reason that Nisei were born in Canada and were therefore not enemy aliens. It was unfair that we were being treated as prisoners of war. We should be regarded as civil prisoners and not potential enemies of the government.

After supper we gathered for some amateur entertainment in the dining room. There was a good variety of singers and dancers. My favourite was K-san, telling us a *naniwa bushi*—a traditional Japanese story. He even had a *sensu*, a Japanese fan, that he fluttered around in long sweeping arcs during his storytelling. The evening was very pleasant.

May 28, 1942

The camp officials exchanged our confiscated money for camp coupons today. We are now able to purchase tobacco, candy, soft drinks, toothpaste, pens, notebooks, and other items from the canteen. A romantic black-and-white motion picture was showing, but it was too hot and stuffy in the dining room to really enjoy it.

Sleeping at night has become almost impossible. The large mosquitoes buzzing and biting in the night's silence make us toss and turn constantly. It is becoming unbearable. We tried to smoke them out by burning wet grass in our tent, but they continued to swarm even when the smoke grew too heavy for us to endure.

May 31, 1942

Today we elected two new Nisei representatives and one tent

leader from each of our tents. Eiichi Yoshikuni was elected as our tent leader. He had been our leader since Hastings Park.

I was surprised earlier today when Abe-san found me in my tent and stopped by to say hello. His face was sunburned behind a large beard; he looked much different than when I had last seen him in Prince Rupert, BC. He held a light frown with his smile, as though he had much on his mind. Abe-san was a good friend of my father's before the war. He has been here since the war began. He got right to the point. He scolded me severely. He said that this was no place for a young man such as myself. That I should take my brother and get out of here as soon as I could. He upset me by saying that I should be helping my parents.

June 2, 1942

We were able to set up another tent to use as a classroom today. Our camp is filled with talented, educated men, all qualified enough to be teachers and instructors. These men have agreed to teach English, Japanese, bookkeeping, handwriting, and music during the time that we are interned together. I am glad to take up some English, Japanese, and bookkeeping lessons.

Since I returned to Canada four years ago, much of my time has been wasted for lack of a formal education. There were so many influences in my life that called upon my youthful desires. It was all too easy to dismiss purpose and succumb to flaccid cravings. I am excited about the chance to learn something that will be useful to me later. There is a small benefit to my imprisonment—now is the time for me to educate myself and lead a more regimented life.

I appreciated the cool breeze that came from an open portion of my tent. Our Japanese class began at 9:30 this morning. I could hardly contain the excitement that I felt as I sat among the men in the makeshift classroom. I sketched while waiting for the lesson to begin and thought upon my past academic life in Japan.

June 4, 1942

Shigeru Kuroyama, one of the men from the original group at the Immigration Building, took ill with appendicitis this morning. He was transported to the military hospital in Port Arthur this morning. We requested to send Dr. Hori, an interned physician along with him, but the camp officials refused.

June 6, 1942

I was having a hard time getting up in the morning. I barely made it in time for breakfast. Perhaps it had something to do with the cool nights and the hot days. If I missed breakfast, I would be forced to wait until lunch for my first meal.

The temperature soared well above one hundred degrees Fahrenheit today. I had never experienced such scorching weather in British Columbia.

June 13, 1942

A commotion occurred among the internees today when they discovered that a young Nisei has been granted release to a sugar beet farm in Alberta. It came as a shock to the Mass Evacuation Movement (MEM) Group that were constantly advocating we should oppose the government's unfair policy together, as a unified whole. Most of us here in Petawawa had voluntarily been interned to protest the evacuation of Japanese Canadians. At any time, any of us can send a written petition to the BC Security Commissioner agreeing to co-operate with the government. It is feared that this individual declaration could eventually weaken the integrity of our protest.

The MEM Group leaders called a meeting to discuss the future prevention of these declarations. The larger part of the Nisei in this concentration camp belong to the Mass Evacuation Movement Group. They represent the remaining Nisei group still living in Vancouver.

Even though we are all in this camp for the same protest, the MEM Group is more concerned with the government's policies of family separations. They believe this to be their primary concern. I later heard that their leaders were clandestinely searching for those men who might be thinking about deserting their cause. I did not know what they would say or do to those men when they found them.

June 15, 1942

I have been in Petawawa for three weeks. Almost every day, the temperature rises above one hundred degrees Fahrenheit. Most of us can only bear to remain within shaded areas during the day. At night the temperature plummets, suddenly leaving the air chill and freezing. It would be some time before I grow accustomed to the drastic temperature changes of this harsh environment.

A meeting was called by some Nisei to discuss a plan to renounce their Canadian citizenship. These men have decided that they have had enough of the Canadian government. To them, it seems to them undignified to be deemed Canadian citizens while imprisoned for their Japanese heritage. In renouncing their Canadian citizenship they hope to nullify their dual citizenship and become Japanese citizens exclusively.

The majority of the camp are against their meeting, since most internees within the camp are party to the Mass Evacuation Movement Group. The slightest hint of opposition is viewed with strong feelings of resentment. They believe that the meeting will pose a threat to them. The MEM Group declared that they would pressure the government until it rescinded the unfair policies imposed on Japanese Canadians. The group maintains that as long as the internees retain their Canadian status, they are entitled to citizen rights and thus retain the honour and liberty to fight for those civil rights.

June 16, 1942
It was cool and cloudy today, a welcome relief from the relentless hot weather. After supper I went to the sand pile on the grounds to practice some wrestling with the men. It is an ideal place to practice as it is spacious and away from camp traffic. By the end of our practice I was happily covered in sand from head to toe.

June 20, 1942
I still have not received any word from my parents. It has now been over a month and a half since we were separated. I have mailed them two letters since being interned but I fear they haven't received them due to government censorship. I will try writing them another letter. With the help of my good friend

Jiro Kiyonaga, I was able (as required by the camp authority) to write my letter in English. I dearly hope they will receive my letter.

In the late afternoon we were ordered to move into a barracks that was formerly occupied by some German POWs. In this sweltering heat, moving was the last thing I felt like doing. I consoled myself with the thought that I would have a solid roof over my head and finally be rid of those maddening mosquitoes. I was completely exhausted by the time I settled into the number ten hut along with the other seventy men. It was almost 7:00 PM and still very hot outside.

June 26, 1942

I awoke to another sunny day. Looking at the familiar clear blue sky revealed that it would be unbearably hot yet again today. Most of the men interned in Petawawa are not accustomed to this hot and humid weather. Even within the shaded buildings, stripped down to our pants, we still feel oppressed by the heavy heat. Outside the sun beats down upon us mercilessly, scorching our skin if we do not take any care to cover up.

A truckload of cull lumber was delivered to our camp this morning. The truck drove off and I rushed over to the woodpile along with some other men. We collected birch bark to use for our artwork. The white birch bark will make a pretty picture frame. We spent the remainder of the day carving and sculpting in the shaded area set behind our barracks.

June 27, 1942

I have yet to hear from my father. I am really starting to worry.

I love him so and will be torn apart if ever anything happens to him. I think very highly of him.

My father was born in 1885, in a small farmhouse in Ichigo, Japan. In 1910, at the age of twenty-five, he was discharged from the Japanese army and emigrated to Canada. He settled down in Skeena River, BC and fished there all of his life. He never once raised his voice. He was a gentle and understanding man. I remember the villagers saying, if you want deer meat, ask Kuwabara; my father was the best deer hunter around. His hobby was to make home-brewed Sake. I guess he was not the best at it, however, because he was constantly testing it until it was all gone. He would get joyful and talkative but he never once showed any sign of drunkenness. He was a simple yet honourable man, and I admired him greatly.

I asked Masago-kun if he could write a letter to his father in Kaslo, BC and ask him to find out what had happened to my beloved parents.

Shortly after lunch, I heard my name called by the mail official. My heart leapt as I ran to the canteen to collect my mail. I glanced at the letter and was glad to see that it was from my father's good friend Fujino-san. The letter was made extremely short due to government censorship. Fujino-san wrote that he was still in Vancouver and was scheduled to be sent out to a road camp any day now.

June 28, 1942

I was busy doing some push-ups, just about ready to go for lunch, when Abe-san stopped by to say hello. I got up and welcomed him. He said he had some important information to share with my brother and me. He told me to go quickly and find my brother, then meet him in his barracks as soon as possible.

I found Shig and we rushed over to meet Abe-san in the number three hut. We sat down together at a table in the centre of the barracks and Abe-san pulled out a letter for us to read. The letter was addressed to Abe-san from Hayakawa-san, who now lived on a sugar beet farm in Manitoba. Hayakawa-san was a very good friend of the family. He had written a letter to Abe-san to ask whether Shig and I had been moved to Petawawa. His query had been made on behalf of my parents. The letter was difficult to read as it had been heavily censored. From what I could tell from the letter, our parents were in Manitoba. I looked at Abe-san and frowned. This new information conflicted with the information Yoshida-san had earlier given us stating that our parents had been relocated to a ghost town in Greenwood, BC. I was anxious and upset. I immediately wrote a letter to Hayakawa-san in Manitoba, requesting further information on the location of our parents.

A SHOOTING INCIDENT

July 1, 1942

I was suddenly awoken in the middle of the night by loud gunshots. I was only half awake but very aware of being in danger. I quickly jumped down from my bunk and flattened myself on the floor. The shots seemed to have come from the watchtowers nearest to the dining area.

A rifle fired another volley of shots. Bang! Bang! Bang! A bullet shattered a nearby window and ricocheted off my bedframe, striking a pillow on the bunk beside me. I looked at the small mushroom-shaped spot on the pillow and was relieved that no one had been sleeping there. It was quiet for a few minutes. I cautiously raised my head to look outside. The tower searchlights were panning all over the grounds; the scene looked like it would soon be a battlefield. I quickly ducked down as I spotted the rifle-holding soldiers in the watchtowers.

I could not bring myself to climb back up on my bunk bed. Even though the shooting had stopped for almost an hour, I feared that it might start again at any moment. I lay motionless on the cold floor, worried and wakeful until dawn.

At daybreak, everyone in the barrack was asking questions about last night's frightening incident. I discovered that the incident had resulted from a meeting that had been called in the dining hall between two Japanese groups. One group was comprised of young Nisei who were trying to be released from the camp, and the others were members of the MEM group who were actively trying to discourage them from leaving.

According to one of the frightened men who had been there, the meeting between the two groups was called for 2:00 AM in the dining hall to avoid any repercussion from the MEM leaders. While they walked towards the dining hall from their hut, the guards turned their watchtower lights on them. Shots were fired from three different directions. The dining hall was their main target but bullets had strayed as far as the adjacent barracks. Bullets had smashed into the kitchen, scattering plates, pots and pans all over the floor.

As the time for the morning roll call approached, a sergeant entered our hut with two armed guards. He ordered us outside. We refused. There was no way we were going to line up for roll call until we had some explanation about what had happened last night, and we told them so. Thus it was that for the first time since our internment, we went without a morning roll call.

Miyazaki-san acted as our chairman and at 10:00 AM the internees in Petawawa assembled before him on the grounds. Tanaka-san, Kobayashi-san, Nishikawa-san, Ishibashi-san, and Endo-san were appointed delegates to inquire about what had caused last night's outrageous shooting incident.

After we had lunched, the camp commander met with our delegates in the guardhouse. Our delegates made a strong protest about the gunfire. They argued that the guards had no right to fire at the internees just because they were moving

around late at night within the compound. The camp commander cut them short. He argued that the men had run out of their
barracks at a suspicious hour, in the early morning. He said that
the guards were completely justified in firing warning shots,
and had simply complied with curfew regulations. At this, our
delegates became furious. How can you say those shots were
warning shots when there are bullet holes throughout the
camp? The camp commander insisted that they had been only
warning shots. Our delegates maintained that they were not
and demanded there be a review of the incident by the Spanish
Consul.

The neutral countries of the war had been appointed by the
Geneva Convention to send consuls to verify that living conditions within POW camps were humane. As a result, a Spanish
Consul visited the Canadian internment and concentration
camps every three months during the war.

Our delegates declared that all of the camp's internees
would refuse to comply with the mandatory roll call order until
the Spanish Consul was allowed to visit. The camp commander
appeared very grim and, without a word, walked out of the
meeting.

Shortly thereafter, the army closed our canteen and suspended all incoming mail, newspapers, and motion pictures.

July 4, 1942

It was unusually overcast this morning. The dark sky reminded
me of Japan's *baiu* rainy season. By noon the sky had begun to
clear.

Three days have passed since our refusal to line up for roll call. Around 4:00 PM a high-ranking official from the Petawawa military headquarters arrived and proposed a meeting with us. Three representatives from each hut met with him at the guardhouse. He admitted to them that the other night's shooting incident was a terrible error. The military should never have fired at the barracks. But this incident had nothing to do with the roll call. Refusal to line up for roll call was a serious offence. If anyone disobeyed this order, the military would be forced to take drastic actions. They would begin by arresting all of our leaders and prosecuting them in a military court of law. Further consequences would follow, even executions if necessary. Our representatives were given no chance to reply when the official suddenly stood up and walked out the door.

Our representatives came back and relayed the message to the anxious crowd that waited on the campgrounds. A loud uproar ensued. After their announcement they left the outraged crowd to meet with our camp leader, Tanaka-san, and discuss this very serious situation: whether to obey the military's order or to continue our protest.

A chubby-faced staff sergeant walked to the front of our crowd, raised his left hand and pointed to his wristwatch, then declared menacingly, "We'll give you internees exactly five minutes to obey our orders to line up for roll call!" With malice in his eyes, he faced the armed soldiers lined up beyond the barbed wire fence.

The time was quickly passing by and nobody said a word. The formation of armed soldiers shifted and suddenly began advancing towards the barbed wire fence. I could almost see the fear in the air, like a curtain of doom dropped between the internees and the soldiers. A cold sweat ran down my underarms when I realized that this was really getting serious. Canadian soldiers shooting Canadians? I never believed it would ever happen, but in that moment I feared that these veteran soldiers would not hesitate to gun down their appointed enemy. They might be thinking that we were war prisoners from the Pacific; some of them might even have resented or hated the Japs. Everyone was pale and frightened. One wrong move from either side would start something unforgettably bloody.

I spotted my brother's timid face in the crowd. My throat made a dry clicking sound as I swallowed. We had been together since childhood. We had suffered many hardships since the time that our mother passed away, but we had always stuck together. We might now die together in this camp. This may very well be the last time I ever see him. The sergeant raised his hand again and said, "Two more minutes to go." Still, nobody moved.

The five-minute deadline came to an end. At that crucial moment, I noticed the grey-haired Tokikazu Tanaka standing amidst the crowd like some long forgotten samurai. He broke away and marched swiftly to the front of the internees. He raised both his hands high in the air and called out to the uneasy crowd in a calm and steady voice, "Gentlemen please, quiet down." He took a deep breath and continued, "Let's line up for roll call."

He walked over to our customary place of roll call. The crowd followed him with apparent relief. Once he saw that everyone had lined up properly, Tanaka-san held his head high and calmly walked towards the gate. He stopped and faced the commanding officer standing beside the formation of soldiers. In a clear voice he reported that the internees were now ready for roll call.

After three days of our stubborn refusal, at 5:15 PM the sergeant major began walking through our ranks, accounting for all the internees. I gave a sigh of relief and gazed at Tanaka-san. I felt proud as I observed his solid poise. I thought to myself, there is the greatest and most courageous man I have ever seen. His calm and courageous action and his great leadership ability had saved us from what was certain to have been a situation of no return.

Ten names were called: Kobayashi, Ishibashi, Matsushita, Yoshikuni, Nishikawa, Nishidera, Oyama, Hayashi, Noda, and Nakagawa. One by one, the guards assembled them to the side before escorting them to a detention room near the gate. They were placed on a military truck. As the truck left the camp, one of the prisoners shouted from the tailgate, "*Ganbare*, don't give up!"

The blazing July sun descended behind the treeline and a cool breeze began to blow gently into our encampment. I was glad that this long day was finally over and very thankful to be alive.

July 7, 1942

We were adjacent to the German POWs and separated only by a barbed wire fence. When the guards were not around, we were able to talk to each other. Since our canteen had been closed, the Germans were supplying us with tobacco, chocolates, oranges and candies. They tossed them over the fence in a show of admiration and sympathy for our courageous roll call standoff.

Members of the Mass Evacuation Movement Group received a report from their headquarters in Vancouver. The report stated that their demands had been partly recognized by the government. All married couples and those single persons who were responsible for taking care of their families were now permitted to move with their families to the relocation centres in the interior of British Columbia. The government promised that all the separated families would be reunited before winter.

The MEM Group felt that since most able-bodied men from the Vancouver area had been removed to the road camps, they did not have sufficient manpower to effectively carry out any further protest against the government. They decided to co-operate with the government for the sake of their families. The news of their decision to end their protest was not received well by many of the internees in Petawawa. They felt let down by the MEM Group.

July 10, 1942

Today the canteen was reopened and mail delivery allowed. I was elated to discover a letter from my parents. In my excitement I forgot what I intended to buy from the canteen and rushed out to find my brother Shig. The letter explained that my parents were safe and had been relocated to Greenwood, BC last month. My father explained that stepmother was adjusting well and that he was kept busy as a carpenter, repairing the old abandoned houses in their new community.

I also received a letter from Hayakawa-san in Manitoba. He confirmed that our parents were living in Greenwood.

I have recently started hiking around the perimeter two or three times every morning. This has become my routine exercise. Sometimes I might take a moment to watch a small squirrel just outside the barbed wire fence, appreciating the sight as it delicately jumps amidst the multitude of tiny white flowers. I walk past the radishes and lettuce that have been sown in a patch of ground by the internees. The fresh vegetables have become our favourite food at dinnertime.

We have had some severe thunderstorms lately. The thunderclouds slowly mushroom in the western sky, condensing upwards from the hot swell of our days. In the late afternoon, the darkness gradually covers our camp. Soon enough we see the lightning flashes, followed by crashing sounds of roaring thunder. Heavy downpours soon follow. Most of the time the storms are short and last only a couple of hours. I revel in the fresh air left behind by the cleansing rain and, marvel at the pristine sight of the surrounding trees. The white poplars are beautiful with their glistening bark and bountiful, lustrous leaves.

The camp commander has given us notice to be prepared for our transportation tomorrow morning. All of the Japanese internees in Petawawa are being relocated to another concentration camp in Angler, Ontario.

Three of the ten men who were arrested after the roll call standoff the other day were released from the Petawawa detention. Nakagawa-san, Oyama-san and Kobayashi-san returned to the camp this afternoon. According to their story, the remaining seven men are to be tried by a military tribunal. I feel very bad for these men, but there is nothing that we can do to help them.

July 20, 1942

We got up at 4:00 AM and were all ready to be transported once again. After a short breakfast of sandwiches, we began the chore of cleaning the compound. At 8:00 AM, 354 internees gathered on the grounds to wait for the trucks to carry us away. I wished I had a camera with me to take some pictures. Men stood and sat together in disarray. Some held boxes and cloth-wrapped packages. An elderly man stood alone, leaning on a homemade cane, with a rolled blanket over his shoulder. The scene reminded me of old folks in Japan preparing to climb Mt. Yomeyama for the shrine festival.

We had not been waiting very long when a convoy of army trucks pulled up to the gate. The German POWs next door were also getting ready to be transported. I heard them shouting, "*Sayonara*" from the trucks as they departed. I waved and silently thanked them for their unexpected friendship.

At 10:00 AM we climbed into the army trucks and departed from Petawawa, accompanied by a heavily armed escort. Inside the crowded truck, pressed together on a wooden seat, I felt like a sardine. So many things had happened in the time since I was interned on April 25, 1942. Three weeks in the Immigration Building, with action-packed days of rioting, shootings and tear-gas, followed by a long train ride to the east, had been very exciting times for me. The camp shooting incident and the roll call standoff had really shown how serious our situation was. There had been so many scary moments and sleepless nights. Through all this unfortunate turmoil, I was most grateful for my brother Shig. When I had most needed it, he had always been there to give me comfort and courage. I was grateful for all the good men at my side. Keeping our heads up though these troubled times had brought us together in a strong brotherhood.

Our convoy of trucks travelled the dusty road we had first travelled only two months ago. After a forty-five-minute road trip, we arrived at the Petawawa train station. Once we were boarded, the train gave a sharp jolt and slowly began to chug towards our distant western destination. Our coaches were much cleaner and newer than the last ones. We were permitted to open the windows a few inches, to allow for some fresh air to breathe. I sat comfortably in the spacious coach with my brother facing me and began to relax.

It felt good to see the outside world passing by in all its different colours. We had been locked behind a barbed wire fence for over two months. The soothing train ride made me feel as if we were on a holiday, all set to relax and enjoy the splendid scenery. Once we had travelled past Sudbury, our train started coasting faster alongside Lake Superior. Shortly after 5:00 PM our train stopped at a small station to allow for another train to pass. Some of the men tried their best to make conversation with a young girl in a short skirt standing on the deserted platform. I could still hear men calling for her as the train began rolling again. We continued our journey west late through the night.

ANGLER CONCENTRATION CAMP

July 21, 1942

An enjoyable nineteen-hour train ride from Petawawa brought us to the Angler Station at 6:15 in the morning. A light fog covered the ground as we disembarked from the train onto the wooden platform. Several armed guards were waiting for us on the nearby gravel road. I remarked how their woollen uniforms were noticeably heavier than the ones the guards had worn back in Petawawa. We marched for three-quarters of a mile, laden with our heavy bags and boxes. As we approached our new camp, my heart sank when I saw the familiar whitewashed huts and barbed wire fence set behind the high watchtowers. Low bushes and high barren hills surrounded the camp, which made for a very dreary view. To the east and south of the camp a detachment of soldiers was encamped within a cluster of whitewashed barracks.

As we entered the concentration camp, the guards thoroughly checked our luggage. We would all be given physical examinations. I stood on the sandy ground for half an hour before my turn came to be examined.

The perimeter of the camp is approximately six hundred metres and is surrounded by two rows of three-metre-high

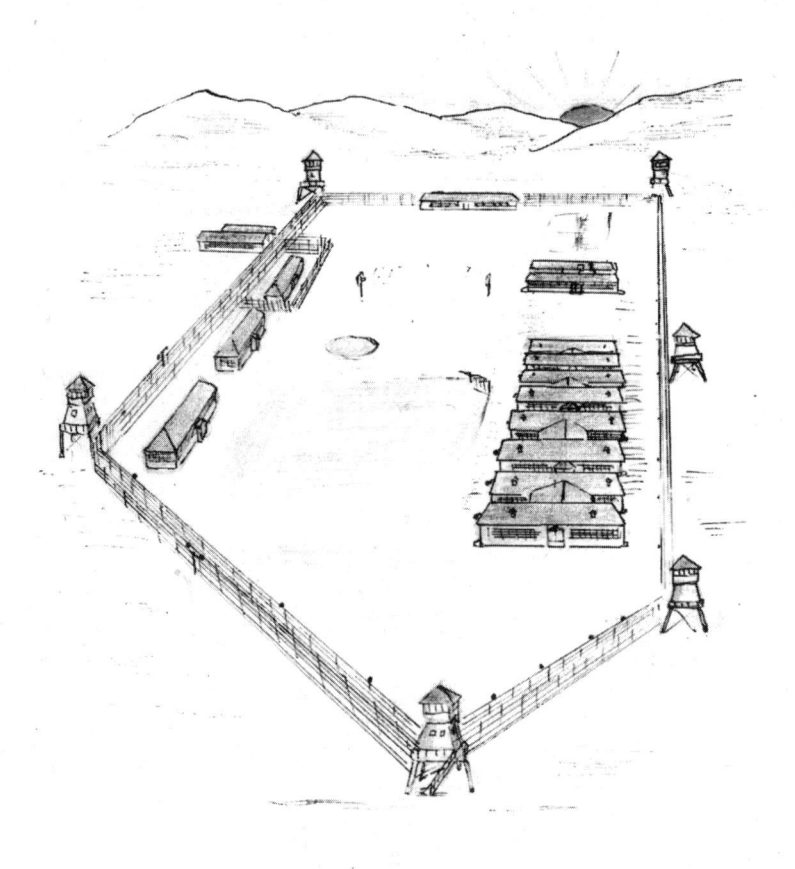

barbed wire fences, a one-metre-high forewarning fence, and six wooden watchtowers. Ten whitewashed barracks are located on the northeast side of the camp. Eight of the barracks are living quarters for the internees. The other two buildings in the northwest of the compound are used as a mess hall and kitchen. The infirmary is set beside the barracks. A detention and guardhouse are located near the gate in the southwest corner. A recreation hall stands alone on the southeast side. The Angler Concentration Camp appears far better equipped for prisoners than Petawawa was.

After my physical examination I was given the inmate registration number 467 and assigned number 5-A hut as my living quarters. Our barracks make up the west wing of an H-shaped building, connected to the neighbouring B-hut by a latrine and laundry facility at the centre. Our A-hut measures approximately six-by-thirty-seven-metres long, and has entrances at the north, south, and east of the building. Inside is a row of twenty army bunk beds that line the east and west walls. Three large cast-iron stoves are firmly set in the centre of the hut.

Some 284 Japanese men are already interned in the camp. Their faces seem very pale and sickly compared to our own dark and sunburned faces. Most of these men are Nisei who supported the protests of the original Mass Evacuation Movement Group interned at Petawawa. Our combined groups number 638 internees.

I have no idea how long this war is going to last. I fear that I might well be in this camp for another three or four, possibly five years. The thought discourages me, but I remind myself that I have made the decision to fight for my rights as a Canadian rather than to be shuffled away unheard and unrecognized. I remind myself of the utmost importance of keeping my mind strong so that I can be at my best while I remain interned at this prison camp.

July 22, 1942

I notice a big difference in the climate here. The cool and cloudy weather in Angler feels like autumn compared to the balmy one hundred degrees back in Petawawa. The morning wake-up call is at 6:30 AM. A guard enters the barracks and chases internees out of bed if they linger for too long. Before going to the mess hall for breakfast, we are required to make our beds with strict military precision. Breakfast-time is split into two shifts, 7:00 and 7:30 AM.

Roll call is held twice a day outside, weather permitting. Minutes prior to roll call, our hut leaders make a quick head count as we line up in three rows at the front of our barracks. At 8:00 AM sharp, a command of "Attention!" begins the strict military roll call. With the sergeant major's loud command— "Six paces forward march!"—a row of internees steps forward and two guards walk between the rows and count the men. It takes over thirty minutes to finish roll call, as there are 638 Japanese internees to be counted. Smoking and talking are prohibited during roll call.

At 11:00 AM an officer and our camp leader, Tanaka-san, enter the barracks to perform an inspection. Whenever an officer is present within the barracks, all the internees are required to remove their caps and silently stand at attention. Lunchtime is at 12:00 noon and 12:30 PM. Suppertime is at 6:00 PM. The evening roll call is held at 9:00 PM. We are strictly prohibited from going out after dark. The lights out time is at 10:00 PM sharp.

One of the internees has mentioned that a guard will be coming around with a flashlight at 1:00 AM to check up on us. I am amazed by the exaggerated protocol of this camp.

July 24, 1942

The cool and cloudy weather continues. Despite being the middle of summer, it feels very much like the end of fall. One of the guards told us that it might go down to sixty below zero in midwinter. I shuffled aimlessly throughout the camp most of the day, searching for something to occupy my time, but could not even find a scrap of wood to work with. I can hardly wait for my next meal, as I am beyond famished, to the point of feeling faint. The canteen doesn't help at all.

July 28, 1942

I sent a telegram to my father in Greenwood to let him know that we have been moved to the Angler camp.

We arrived here last week and have yet to receive all of our belongings. Most of us do not have any books to read or anything at all to occupy our time with. Our inadequate diet leaves us feeling hungry. We anxiously watch the time go by. The camp commander issued an order for sixty more men to carry the camp's rations by hand from the train station. The internees are also required to take out the garbage, clean the army barracks, and unload the coals from the train, all on an empty stomach.

A guard informed me that the reason for the extra security is on account of the former residents of this camp. The German POWs had constructed a radio out of empty tobacco cans. They had also made a tunnel beneath the barbed wire fences and used wooden boards they had found under the bunkhouses as a bracing material. Four of them were shot dead while trying to escape. Some of the prisoners had succeeded in escaping and made it as far as Saskatchewan before they were captured.

July 29, 1942

I joined a work crew today. I went out with eight men to unload coal from the boxcars at the train station. We were designated the coal party. We were three men to a car and were each given a big square shovel to haul coal from the dark and dirty boxcars. We worked hard for a while in the car and came out to catch our breath, nearly asphyxiated from the coal dust. In no time at all, a guard came around and chased us back into the boxcar again. We worked from 8:30 AM until 4:00 PM, with a one-and-a-half-hour lunch break. At the end of the day we were all very tired and hungry. No one said a word as we slowly dragged ourselves back to camp.

July 31, 1942

Some of the men came back to the camp quite angry yesterday. They were saying that they had been forced to work at gunpoint after an argument broke out with the guards.

Our spokesman brought it up with the staff sergeant in charge of the work crews. Tanaka-san informed him that as of yesterday's gun-prodding incident, none of us were willing to work. The sergeant pleaded for us to go back to work and apologized for what had happened. He said that the coal was needed for the cold winter months and promised that it would never happen again.

August 1, 1942

We have finally been allowed to retrieve some of our luggage from the camp's storage warehouse. But we were forbidden from taking any of the cans, medication, and civilian clothing from our luggage. I was happy to recover some of my reading and writing materials.

I am gaining more confidence within this new camp. I am feeling more at ease. I have become more acquainted with the men around me and am slowly growing accustomed to my setting.

August 4, 1942

We held a meeting this afternoon to discuss some of the concerns we will share with the Spanish Consul who is expected to visit our camp sometime today. After supper, only the Issei, first-generation Japanese Canadians, were permitted to meet with the Spanish Consul in the recreation hall. It seemed most unfair that the Nisei were denied the right to see him. I do not expect much will come out of this meeting.

August 5, 1942

It was unusually warm and clear today, the warmest day in all the time I have been here. In the afternoon, we held a baseball tournament between the pre-Petawawa and pre-Angler internees. All of us were out cheering for our team players. It was a lot of fun. More fun than any of us have had in a long time.

After supper Tanaka-san gave us a report of yesterday's meeting with the Spanish Consul. The Issei members had asked the Consul to issue a formal request to Japan for more support for the Japanese nationals and their families living in Canada. Among the list of concerns presented to the Consul was the shortage of food in the camp, our refusal to work because of the way we are treated, our concern for the seven men arrested in Petawawa, and the proposed renouncement of citizenship by some of the Japanese internees.

The Spanish Consul told Tanaka-san that support from the Japanese government is already on its way. The Consul will consult directly with the Canadian government regarding the safety and welfare of Japanese families.

He further said that a prisoner exchange ship has already transported a cargo of rice and *shoyu* from Japan. This shipment of food will arrive any day now. This might solve some of the food problems in the camp but, regardless, the food shortage in the camp is unusual and will be immediately raised with the camp commander.

The camp's maintenance orders must be followed. All internees have to attend to their work duties, regardless. Military officials will be approached with regards to the seven men who were detained in Petawawa a month ago. Any Nisei under the age of twenty with parents who are Japanese nationals will be given the right to renounce their citizenship. Otherwise, Canadian-born Nisei are to remain as Canadians as long as they reside in Canada.

In closing, the Consul said he was doing his best to protect the interest of those Japanese nationals who are in Canada. He also said, with some regret, that Canadian-born Nisei are outside his jurisdiction. He has been appointed by the Geneva Convention to investigate only those concerns regarding the international community. All internal politics are none of his affair.

Upon hearing this final statement, I felt at a loss. Betrayed by motherland Canada and abandoned by fatherland Japan, I had nowhere to turn.

August 10, 1942

All day, I could hear an eerie howling noise outside. An untamed wind gusted wildly though the barbed wire fences, stirring a mighty cloud of sand raised high up above our camp.

At noon, five delegated internees—Tanaka-san, Oyama-san, Fujii-san, Akiyama-san, and Ebisuzaki-san—were transported to Petawawa. They will be attending a hearing on behalf of the seven men arrested in Petawawa. I hope that all goes well for the seven men.

August 11, 1942

The wind settled down today. It was my turn to be on the work crew again. A guard escorted three of us to empty the garbage cans. We followed a garbage wagon for about three-quarters of a mile to the garbage pit. Once we had completed our work duty, we asked the friendly guard to take us to the site where the German POWs had been buried.

We climbed the south side of a grassy hill and found four wooden crosses set within a small wooden fence. German names along with their military serial numbers and ages were cut into the white crosses. All three had been twenty-one years old. We gathered some wild daisies and red flowers from the nearby field and laid them on their graves. We prayed for these young men who are buried within this remote wilderness, so many thousands of miles away from their homeland. From there we climbed further up the hill and sat looking down at the vast, watery scene of Lake Superior.

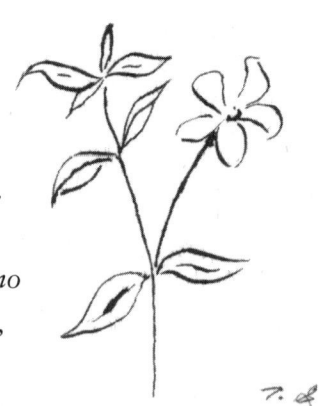

Four crosses stand,
Among the wildflowers
On the evening-shadowed,
Lonely hillside.

Angler *no*
yukaze sabishi jujika no oka,
Shojo to nogiku saki chiru.

August 21, 1942

The small group that had recently left for the Petawawa hearing returned today. They spoke well of the hearing, saying that the seven men had been tried in a military court of law and that things seemed to be in their favour. They would be released from their detainment and arrive at Angler in a short time.

We received a message from the camp commander that a prisoner exchange ship from Japan was on its way to New York. Some of the Issei internees are overjoyed at the news that they may have a chance to return to Japan. Other older Nisei and members of the Canadian Citizenship Renouncement Group are also excited by the news. N-san and O-san, leaders of the CCR Group, began collecting the names of the internees who want to be repatriated to Japan.

August 28, 1942

After two days of steady rain, it finally cleared up nicely this morning. Still, the clear emerald sky and cool north wind make me think that fall and winter were soon approaching.

N-san and O-san brought up the Canadian citizenship renouncement issue again, advocating their views to some of the internees in the camp. There was fervent opposition from the Mass Evacuation Movement Group and an argument broke out between several internees. The commotion abated after a while, but I suspect that there may be further disagreements between the two groups in the future.

August 30, 1942

A group of forty-six Japanese internees arrived from the Immigration Building in Vancouver this afternoon. The majority of these men are Issei in their thirties and forties. Most of these men were imprisoned because of their willful opposition to the Canadian government. They have come from the road camps near Slocan, BC, and look like weary Japanese soldiers, their faces sunburned and hair shortly cropped.

Some of them openly admit that they are more than unsatisfied with the Mass Evacuation Movement Group. They feel that the group is bowing to the government's demands. They say that if the group was formed to represent Japanese Canadians, the group should be resolutely standing its ground and fighting for all of our rights as Canadians.

September 1, 1942

We held a memorial service for the Kanto disaster in Japan.

After the morning roll call, we faced east and said a traditional prayer for the Japanese people who suffered so long ago.

Standing silently together, I thought about our place in this endless world war. The world is caught in a struggle for domination. I feel like a small mouse caught in the middle of an agonizing war. It is up to me now to pull through these uncertain times. I have to keep my head above the turbulent waves and make for certain shores: in my heart, I know this is true.

September 3, 1942

I was surprised to see frost on the doorsteps and the rooftops this morning. It is only the beginning of September and the freezing wind feels like the beginning of January.

I was scheduled to be on the work crew again today. Six of us left the camp with a guard to unload coal from a boxcar. A month ago there were all kinds of wildflowers in full bloom along the roadside. Today, the flowers look like white, matted fur, frozen solid under a carpet of morning frost. In the distance I could see a few wild daisies still standing here and there.

Angler's short-lived summer had gone,
　　　　With cold north wind,
Only some wild daisies stand bravely,
　　　　On the lonely field,

　　Natsu sugite kitakaze samushi
　　　　　Angler no,
　　Sunahara ni saku nogiku ooshi.

THE CITIZENSHIP
RENOUNCEMENT MOVEMENT

September 12, 1942

Some of the internees have begun sending application forms to the Minister of Justice asking to renounce their Canadian citizenship. The whole camp is consumed with noisy arguments between the newly formed Canadian Citizenship Renouncement Group and the Mass Evacuation Movement Group.

The Canadian Citizenship Renouncement Group proclaim that since the beginning of the war, Japanese Canadians have been severely mistreated by the Canadian government. They maintain that they were stripped of all democratic rights as Canadian citizens the moment their assets were seized, and were now regarded as enemy aliens imprisoned in a wilderness area far from civilization. To them, it made no sense to retain their citizenship.

They were determined to renounce their Canadian citizenship immediately and become Japanese citizens exclusively. They would be better off, they claimed, as true Japanese nationals, rather than being pseudo-Canadians. They argued that even if they were to remain in Canada after the war and became model Canadian citizens, the government would still look down at them as yellow-faced Japs and treat them like second-class citizens, just as it had done before the war.

They seemed confident saying that Japan was now much different from what it was a year ago. The vast territories of south Asia and the south Pacific are now under Japanese occupation. These lands are filled with opportunities for anyone loyal to Japan. It seems pointless for them to remain in this "hard-up country, Canada."

The Mass Evacuation Movement Group is firmly opposed to their position. During these trying times, the group's immediate objective is to secure the Japanese community's welfare. They said that the Canadian Citizenship Renouncement Movement will undermine their efforts by worsening the government's ill feelings towards the Japanese community. As long as the Japanese Nisei retain their citizenship they will have the right to voice their protests against the government's atrocious policies.

As the days went by, the animosity between these two groups grew noticeably fierce. Most of the older Issei try not to get involved in the heated debate. They sympathize and remain neutral towards both groups, believing that all arguments are equally justified.

September 15, 1942

The seven men detained in Petawawa arrived at our camp this afternoon. A crowd of internees was waiting to welcome them at the gate. Matsushita-san, Hayashi-san, Ishibashi-san, Noda-san, Yoshikuni-san, Nishikawa-san, and Nishidera-san marched into Angler with a proud and steady pace. Although somewhat pale and fatigued, they appeared to be in fairly good shape for having been confined to a cell for the past seventy-three days.

Yoshikuni-san informed us that the first three weeks of confinement within the small prison cell had been terribly hard, but he had set his mind to cope with the harshness of the situation and his imprisonment had soon become much easier. After a while, he learned to exercise in the small area and played *Shogi* as a form of entertainment with the other men. In the time of his confinement, he was most grateful for all the letters of support he received from his family and friends.

September 20, 1942

It was an unseasonably cold morning with a light frost covering the ground and rooftops. This looks to be a short-lived fall as winter rapidly covers the land. The trees surrounding the camp are already changing to yellow and orange, leaving the scattered evergreens to appear more prominent in our Angler setting.

In the afternoon we held an entertainment event in the recreation hall. It was the first indoor entertainment we have had in Angler. It was a wonderful feeling to see all the internees participating in a friendly, carefree atmosphere.

I was overjoyed later in the day when I received a letter from my good friend Yoshikazu Tani. I recalled the good times Yoshikazu and I had spent together in Skeena River. We both lost our mothers when we were small boys, and were both brought up by our relatives in different parts of Japan. We had returned to Canada together four years ago on the same ship, the *Princess of Asia*. We had fished the coastal waters near our

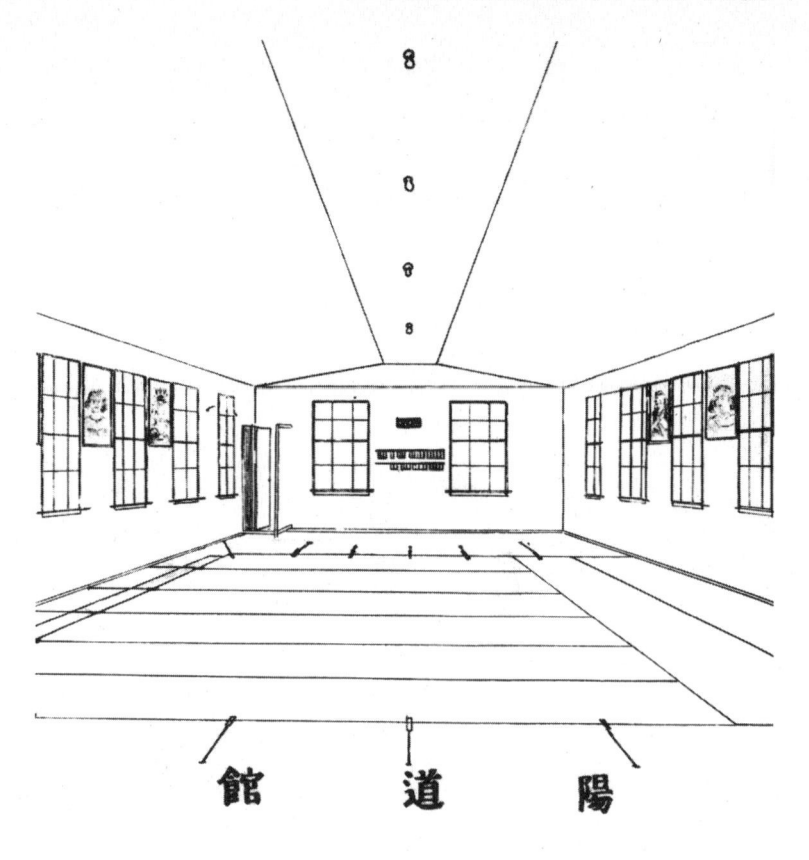

West Coast village together, in loving friendship for four years.
He was like a brother to me.

September 30, 1942

The cool and cloudy weather has continued for several days.
Some light snow fell the other day and still remains within the
covered areas. Today seems warmer, or perhaps I am just getting used to the cool weather.

Recently the internees have been changing their minds
about their pleas for early release. There is a rumour in the

camp that a Nisei group in Vancouver is negotiating with the government to release some of the internees from Angler.

More arguments have ensued between several of the internees. The camp grows more divided by differing opinions and enmity every day. The Mass Evacuation Movement Group is still advocating family unity, but they are rapidly losing support. Some of the members have decided that the MEM group is doing a poor job, and that they would be better off disassociating themselves from the group.

October 9, 1942

I wrote another letter to my parents. I informed them that my brother and I are in good health, trying our best to occupy ourselves within our life of internment. The most enjoyable time in this camp is reading our mail and corresponding with our distant friends and relatives.

We have had some warm weather this past week. One of the guards told us it was an "Indian summer." Our sunsets are exceptionally beautiful. The setting sunlight reflects pink and crimson colours upon the elongated clouds, floating in the distant western skies. I watched large purple clouds above me as I waited for the evening roll call to be over. The clouds turned dark blue as they slowly moved towards the eastern skies.

October 10, 1942

A Spanish Consul made an unofficial visit to our camp late last night. When the Consul entered our hut during the morning inspection, our representatives handed him our requests. As usual, only the Issei were allowed to see him. The Consul told them that the shipment of *shoyu*, rice and other materials from Japan had been held up at the Canada inspections office. Some eighteen Japanese men from our camp are officially scheduled to be deported to Japan, as requested.

October 15, 1942

It was another nice day. The so-called Indian summer has continued for well over a week. Our long-awaited academic classes commenced today. Thanks to the determined efforts of several volunteers, we are now able to study Japanese, English, bookkeeping, shorthand writing, music, and more.

October 18, 1942

All the leaves have fallen to the ground, exposing the bare branches of the deciduous trees that surround our camp. Dark-green conifers can be seen here and there on the lonely mountainsides and nearby hills.

We held another entertainment activity in the dining hall this morning, to honour the seven men who were released from Petawawa. It is a time of peace among the 690 internees.

The event opened with a passionate speech by our camp leader Tanaka-san. Matsushita-san followed with an overstated speech about his personal sacrifices in remaining a true Canadian. A guarded silence clouded the hall for a moment after he sat down. Then a variety of performances began. There was a *naniwa bushi* (Japanese storyteller), singers, some harmonica music, and many more events that lasted until 4:00 PM.

It was an enjoyable afternoon, but Matsushita-san's harsh criticism of the Canadian Citizenship Renouncement Group caused unnecessary tension. I felt that it had been somewhat inappropriate.

October 21, 1942

At 1:00 PM, 130 members of the Canadian Citizenship Renouncement Group met in the dining hall to protest Matsushita-san's controversial speech. They demanded an explanation. Tanaka-san arranged to have Matsushita-san apologize for having overstated his opinions. Everyone seemed happy and went back to their huts.

By the time we had finished our evening roll call, a bitter northerly wind had descended from the mountains to the fields and into our camp. I could sense that the hidden snow, gathering in the cloudy sky above would fall any day.

October 22, 1942

I was assigned to a work crew again today. In the mornings, four of us followed a guard out of the camp. Our job was to dig a hole for a garbage pit about three-quarters of a mile from the camp.

Small snowflakes fell from the sky as we passed through the gate. By the time we reached the tool shed in the army barracks, the gently falling snow had turned into a blinding snowstorm. In no time at all, everything around me had changed into a blank backdrop. I stood watching the big snowflakes descend from the skies above and was reminded of a harsh North Pole scene I had once seen in a motion picture.

After three hours of work at the garbage pit, we returned to the camp in time for lunch. It had stopped snowing but it seemed that we would be in this wintry land for a while yet.

After supper I overheard a sad quarrel coming from the neighbouring hut. Apparently, T-san had discovered that his son, without his consent, had made an application to leave the camp. Both of them had come to this camp as members of the Mass Evacuation Movement Group. Now his son had changed his mind and secretly made plans to leave the camp along with some other young men. Fearing certain objection, he had not mentioned any of this to his father.

I sympathized with T-san's pain, having discovered that his son was willing to abandon him for a few new friends. I was saddened when I saw his tear-stained face and heard his trembling voice. Some friends came over and calmed the situation down a little. They tried to talk the son into being more respectful towards his father and to continue with the hard choices they had made together. I listened to their words but thought they would be in vain.

October 30, 1942

It was drizzling lightly this morning. It reminded me of Japan's early spring, the time of melting snow. The mountains on the north side of the camp were hazy silhouettes in the misty rain.

None of us felt like going to work in this nasty weather, but still we were forced to go out to dig the garbage-pit. By the time we finally reached the job site, we were all soaking wet. We returned to the camp, not having done any work. It continued to rain heavily all afternoon. When I left my bunkhouse for supper, the snow on the ground had almost completely washed away.

I was happy to receive a letter from my parents today. My father wrote that they are still doing well, working hard to repair the makeshift buildings in their community. He provided us with a few recent photographs. I was relieved when I saw how healthy their faces appeared in the pictures. But seeing them smiling together made me feel sad.

November 1, 1942

We received part of the consolation shipment from the Japanese Red Cross Society today. The packages arrived with the exchange ship, *Green Hornet*, from Japan about a month ago. There were all kinds of Japanese foods: *shoyu, miso,* rice and 150 pounds of Japanese tea. The arrival of the shipment raised a loud cheer throughout the camp. For supper we enjoyed filling ourselves with salted salmon and some dear, fragrant Japanese tea. I wholeheartedly thanked the people of Japan for having given us such a commendable gift.

November 3, 1942

The weather has been cold and cloudy since the last snowfall. It was nice to see the early sunlight shining through my window when I awoke this morning. I walked across the frost-covered ground towards the mess hall and saw the faint sickle moon slightly tilted in the twilight sky. I shivered in the cold. Winter has arrived to stay.

At 1:00 PM all the internees gathered in the recreation hall to celebrate the *Meiji Setsu* (the Emperor Meiji's birthday). We sang "*Kimi ga yo,*" which was followed by Tanaka-san's graceful speech. After the ceremony, the hall was filled with a variety of entertainment. We forgot about our differences of opinion and enjoyed the rest of the afternoon in a friendly atmosphere.

November 9, 1942

Twenty men left the camp today. They were sent to a bush camp near Port Arthur, Ontario, with the hopes of someday being reunited with their families. Recently, it seems that more men are applying for a release from the camp.

I overheard a few young men gathered in the west-side corner of our hut, very quietly discussing their plans to leave the camp. They are considering the possibility of being released from Angler. Most of them are willing to abandon their protests and sign an agreement of co-operation with the Canadian government. Later on, one of the young men from the west side came over to the east side of our hut, where most of the *ganbari ya* lived, and casually started to say something in English. I then heard a loud shout from a *ganbari ya* commanding that if the young man was Japanese, he had better speak Japanese. This was an unusual circumstance, yet it demonstrated the tension between the men who wanted to depart and the men who wanted to remain loyal to their protest.

November 10, 1942

Early this morning I was awakened by a fierce rattling noise at the window. The entire building was shaking as though it was ready to break apart and blow away. A gale-force blizzard was ripping through the camp. I barely made it to the dining hall for breakfast as the strong north wind blew across the field and sent blinding snow into my face. The blizzard lasted all morning and slowly tapered off by the afternoon.

I wrote a letter to Aunt Orui and my stepbrother Fukuji in Japan. I do not know when or if the letter will reach Japan.

November 12, 1942

There were three or four inches of snow on the ground when I awoke this morning. The snow is sure to remain as the ground is now frozen solid.

When we heard that a group of internees were on their way from the Immigration Building in BC, the internees moved their beds closer to their friends. All the men who planned to co-operate with the government moved to the west side of our hut and the *ganbari ya* moved to the east side. Our hut was now split into two definite groups, with a neutral party occupying the centre of the hut. The animosity between the two opposing groups was clearly getting worse.

At around 3:00 PM a group of fifty-six new internees arrived. Most of the men were in their mid-thirties. According to their story, they had been detained within the Immigration Building for over two months until finally being transported to Angler. No one had gone to visit them, as nearly all Japanese had been evacuated from the Vancouver area. They reported that a group of over forty Japanese women and children who had refused to co-operate were still being detained within the Immigration Building.

November 16, 1942

Yoshida-san is one of the newly arrived internees and a member of the Mass Evacuation Movement Group in Slocan, BC.

He reported to the MEM Group leader today, stating that as of September 15, the relocation of all Japanese Canadians in the BC coast area had been completed. The MEM Group headquarters has been moved to the ghost town areas. There is now a severe shortage of houses in the overpopulated relocation settlements. Many families are forced to live in tents. Internees are outraged by the report. They feel bad that they are powerless to help their families, now forced to survive in tents in the middle of winter.

The newly arrived internees gave us an update on the war in the Pacific. The American fleet has maintained a defensive position in the South Pacific. The Japanese Empire has superior naval power in the Solomon Islands. The Japanese battleship *Haruna* was reported sunk in the Philippine Sea, but she was later sighted at the battle of Midway.

November 17, 1942

Members of the Citizenship Renouncement Movement Group were angered by the report presented by Yoshida-san. They furiously declared that the Mass Evacuation Movement Group from the ghost town areas should mind their own business concerning the release of internees from Angler. Members of the CRM Group maintain that they are not willing to negotiate a release with the government as long as the government maintains its unfair policies towards Japanese Canadian people. The group declared that from this point onwards, no other address will be made to the Mass Evacuation Movement Group.

Sometime after the CRM Group had finished its public declaration, a meeting with the leaders of the Mass Evacuation

Movement Group was proposed. They met in the recreation hall. A spokesman from the CRM Group informed the MEM Group leaders that the CRM Group would no longer recognize the MEM Group. This final address to the MEM group was followed by a short, vehement speech by O-san that stated all the reasons for their secession from the group and pointed out the weaknesses and inadequacies of the MEM Group from its very beginning in Vancouver. The Citizenship Renouncement Group would now follow its own agenda.

After many months of adversity and arguments, those men from the Citizenship Renouncement Group who had been loyal to the Mass Evacuation Movement Group from the very beginning departed from the MEM Group.

NEW YEAR IN ANGLER

January 1, 1943

A new year had arrived in our snow-covered camp. The white-capped mountains shone with a silver brilliance under the pale morning moon. It was six in the morning and still very dark. The air was clear and still. Snow creaked under my boots as I walked on the frozen ground, the crisp sound echoing sharply on the walls of the surrounding barracks.

Happy New Year! I murmured pensively. A mighty minus-thirty-degree chill crept into my body. I glanced at the frozen moon as I opened the door leading to the mess hall. I was now twenty-two years old according to the Japanese calendar, which accounted for birthdays on the first day of the year. New Year's Day felt no different from any other day in this camp. We wore the same uniforms and had the same food on our plates. The only noticeable difference was that the internees who gathered by the stoves were heartily exchanging greetings and talking about last year's occurrences.

The past year had been the stormiest, most perilous year of my life. I doubted that such an adventurous year could ever occur again. I divided my past year into three phases. From the start of the Pacific war on December 7, 1941 to March 1942 had been a fairly calm period. I somberly awaited my fate, guided mostly by rumours of uncertainty. April 1942 to September 1942 was the most turbulent period. An explosive riot sent me on a train ride to Petawawa where I was part of a terrifying shooting incident. A tense standoff with the army authorities had clearly demonstrated the perilous nature of my welfare. Finally, a comfortable train ride had transported me to the icy domain of the Angler concentration camp. From September 1942 to the end of that year had been a slow period of hibernation.

My mind and body had become accustomed to the routine of living in the camp; my nerves were calmed and my self-worth had started to return. There had been many excitable occurrences in the camp, such as the Canadian Citizenship Renouncement Movement, the Mass Evacuation Movement and all those internees who abandoned their protest to leave the camp. But I had learned how to be reserved in my own beliefs and not to become entangled in adversity and disputes. I was calm in these turbulent times yet, like a dormant volcano, a burning fire smouldered deep within me, waiting patiently to be released.

The year 1942 was a very uncertain and heartbreaking year for the Japanese community. It was a shocking experience for a young man such as myself. Before the war, there had been almost nothing for me to worry about. Living at my parents', my greatest responsibility had been helping my father with fishing. It was a very different time now. I had to make my own decisions and watch out for myself. My brother provided me with much encouragement and was good company, but as he was younger I had to come up with my own sound advice.

I was not bitter about all that had happened to me over the last year. My life had been made more difficult, to the point of being perilous, yet the harsh conditions had made me stronger. The explosive situations and hostile differences I had witnessed had taught me how to adapt and make important decisions concerning my well-being. This past year had shown me who I really was and how important it was for me to stand for my heritage as a true Canadian Nisei.

The Japanese Canadian families today were greeting the New Year in an altogether different manner from a year ago. I imagined my parents in Greenwood, BC, huddled together in a roughly decorated room—a poorly insulated shack, really, that had been constructed for burly miners—sitting alone at the New Year's table, politely talking about my brother and me. I had no way to arrange a *kagezen* (a meal for an absent person) in this concentration camp, but I offered a small plate of cookies to my parents' picture and prayed for their good health. They looked so very lonely together, as they smiled at me from the picture.

Before lights out, I sat down and wrote some of my New Year's resolutions:

– I will stick to the beliefs I reason to be the best.

– I will not allow my mind to become distracted from my reasoning.

– Once I start a project, I will finish it.

– I will not start something that I feel has no chance of being completed.

– My resolutions will be carried out immediately.

A lonely New Year,
My parents smile
lonely
In their picture on the desk,
Where I write my diaries.

Nikki kaku tsukue ni
sonaeshi ryoshin no,
Shashin hohoemi shogatsu sabishi.

January 5, 1943

It was a little warmer today. The sky was overcast and it looked like it might snow later. Our study classes commenced again yesterday. I was studying Japanese writing, English, and bookkeeping.

We received a New Year's greeting from the Japanese government foreign ministry through the International Red Cross Society.

January 9, 1943

The temperature has stayed warm, even as the overcast and snowy weather continues. We can all finally breathe easier in this above-thirty-degree weather.

The camp has grown very quiet as no one is being released, perhaps on account of the cold weather. I expect that more men will be released once the warmer weather arrives. We have received a large amount of cigarettes and some delicious cakes from Roseberry, BC.

January 10, 1943

About two months ago, under the instructions of Okubo-san, a former Japanese sergeant, my brother and I, along with forty young men, began practicing a strict, military-style training program. These bitterly cold winter days have not stopped our dedication to marching and running alongside the barbed wire fence. We practice twice a day, morning and afternoon, with unyielding devotion. Even the minus-thirty-degree weather cannot stop us. Our eyebrows and eyelashes covered with frost, icicles hanging from our noses—still, we continued to run.

Upon completing our run, we assemble for one hour in the recreation hall to practice some Japanese military marching drills. Some of the internees say that our youth group shouldn't practice the Japanese military drills in front of the Canadian guards. The criticism does not bother us because we know that Okubo-san is training us to increase our mental concentration and save our minds and bodies from the debilitating lethargy of this camp.

Tanaka-san gave our Young Men's Training Group an encouragement speech today, after our training session was completed in the recreation hall. He said that the strength of a nation can be measured by how the young men of the nation are living. He emphasized that someday we may become world leaders. Our Japanese race now has the power to unify the world. As the young men of our race, we should be at our healthiest at all times. "Keep training young men and improve yourself for the needs of the coming year," he said. I truly appreciate his provocative words of wisdom.

January 14, 1943

It snowed all day. Big cotton-like snowflakes fell from the ashen sky, reminding me once again of my winters in Japan. Our nice skating rink is now completely buried in snow.

At around 4:00 PM another seventeen internees arrived from the Immigration Building in Vancouver. They were mostly middle-aged men. They told us that the remaining women and children held at the Immigration Building had been taken away before they left. They seemed very upset that they did not know exactly where the women and children had been taken to.

January 18, 1943

The temperature dropped to almost minus fifty degrees this morning. It has been the coldest day this winter so far. I had a very hard time getting to the dining hall for breakfast. The dry cold air felt like a hundred needles piercing my exposed skin as I walked stiffly across the frozen grounds.

We are compelled by the cold to remain in our dingy bunkhouses. Deprived of any fresh air or exercise, cold symptoms have begun to spread among the internees. Some of the men suffering cold sweats and high fevers remain in their bunk beds, as there are not enough aspirins or beds for them in the infirmary.

January 27, 1943

The director of the International Red Cross Society visited us today. Tanaka-san accompanied Dr. Ernest L. Marg and gave him some information about our living conditions as he inspected the camp compound. They met in the presence of the camp commander from 11:00 AM to 4:00 PM. After the meeting, Dr. Marg gave us a New Year's greeting message from the Japanese Red Cross Society.

I appreciate the frequent contact from the Red Cross Society. It is encouraging to know that we are not completely isolated from the rest of the world.

January 28, 1943

We received a detailed report from Tanaka-san today with regards to yesterday's meeting. As requested by the Japanese government, the director of the International Red Cross Society, Dr. Marg, has completed a thorough inquiry into the living conditions within the Angler concentration camp. He had arrived here after carrying out a similar inspection tour of the Japanese relocation areas in British Columbia.

Several items were brought to his attention. Tanaka-san requested that the camp infirmary be improved, along with a better supply of medications. Dr. Marg inquired about the number of illnesses in the camp and Tanaka-san replied that colds are common, as the climate is disagreeable to the internees, accustomed as they are to the warmer climate of British Columbia. Tanaka-san then suggested that all of the internees in the camp be relocated to another camp with a better climate.

Dr. Marg agreed to consult with the Canadian government on the funeral expenses of the late Takahashi-san, who died eight months ago at the Winnipeg General Hospital.

When Tanaka-san asked Dr. Marg's opinion about the shooting incident at Petawawa six months ago, the commander instantly objected to the question, saying that this was strictly a military matter that could not be discussed. Dr. Marg frowned at the objection and made a note of it.

The men in the camp want more rice. The commander's assistant said that this request will be considered. Tanaka-san is opposed to the midnight inspections. The sound of the guards' footsteps and the glare of the bright flashlights are disturbing to some of the internees. He also asked that an investigation be carried out into the whereabouts of the thirty-six missing Japanese women and children who had been interned in the Immigration Building and recently removed to an unknown destination. Dr. Marg said he would investigate this matter immediately.

Once our requests had been made, Dr. Marg reported on some of his findings from his recent investigation of Japanese relocation centres in BC.

The evacuation of all Japanese Canadians from Vancouver and the BC coastal region is complete. No Japanese men, women or children remained in the Immigration Building at the time of his inspection. Some 2,644 Japanese evacuees are now residing in the vicinity of Tashme. About six hundred men are working, receiving an average wage of twenty-two cents an hour. Those who are not working receive eleven dollars a month from a government relief fund. Most families are having a hard time coping with the insufficient sum of money. Yasutaro Yamada-san from Tashme, number eleven camp, informed him that almost everyone is working for twenty-two cents an hour. There was no other complaint from the Tashme Relocation Centre.

About twelve hundred elderly men, women, and children

are living in the Greenwood area. A Reverend Katsuno mentioned to Dr. Marg that the area suffers from overcrowding and a crippling dampness. Over the past year the community had established a hospital. Many families receive an insufficient living allowance from the government's relief fund. Most of their food supply consists of vegetables grown in their own gardens.

Wealthier Japanese families were given the choice of living in the Grand Forks Relocation Centre. Only three per cent of these families receive support from the government relief fund. (The government allows them to withdraw money from their own bank accounts.) Their representative, Sataro Isoya-san, reported that the excessive dampness in the area is disagreeable.

Katsutoro Tanaka-san and Shigeichi Uchibori-san represent the Lemon Creek relocation area. They are in need of additional relief funds from the government. They will gladly accept a supply of food instead of additional government funding. Dampness in the houses is having an adverse affect on some of the newer evacuees who complain of difficulty of breathing and sore joints. The Lemon Creek Hospital is being run very efficiently by a Taiwanese native, Dr. Sae. Dr. Marg was so impressed by the facility that he sent a special provision to the Japanese government commending Dr. Sae's exceptional work.

S. Kondo-san reported that all twelve hundred Japanese evacuees in the New Denver area are in good health.

At Roseberry, J. Wakabayashi-san reported that half of the four hundred evacuees are working and the other half are living impoverished lives, receiving only the insufficient government relief. The community seems very happy about a school that they recently built.

T. Sugiura-san interpreted for Reverend Katazuma in the Sandon area. About nineteen hundred evacuees are in need of relief money and more vegetable seeds are requested for their gardens.

At Kaslo, BC, Tadashi Sudo-san requested more relief funds for the one thousand evacuees living in the area. A hospital is well looked after by Dr. Shimotakahara. While Dr. Marg was inspecting the relocation centre, a woman named Shizue Kamishiro approached him and asked him to find out if her husband Fumio Kamishiro is interned in Angler. She had a message for her husband, that he should try to stay in the camp until the end of the war.

Once Dr. Marg's substantial report was completed, the supervised meeting fell into a more relaxed conversation. The camp commander informed Dr. Marg that Tanaka-san's request to relocate the internees to a better climate was presently being considered by the government. Dr. Marg looked briefly at his notes and shook his head. He concluded to the camp commander that, having made a thorough inspection of the Japanese relocation areas in British Columbia, Canadians living in the Japanese-occupied countries of Asia were receiving far better treatment than were the Japanese Canadians living in Canada.

After the meeting, Dr. Marg wrote down the names of all 661 Japanese men interned in Angler. Presently, there were 397 Nisei, 206 Japanese nationals, 55 Kikajins (naturalized Canadians), and three Japanese Hawaiians. He recorded the names and locations of the more than one hundred Japanese men who had been released from the camp. He also recorded the names of those Japanese men who have applied for their

Canadian status to be renounced. He then wrote down at length the present conditions within our camp. His report is to be sent directly to the Japanese government.

At the close of the five-hour meeting, Tanaka-san thanked Dr. Marg on behalf of the Angler internees for his lengthy visit.

January 29, 1943
An official from the BC Security Commission was here to promote some employment opportunities for those wanting to leave the camp.

According to some news reports, the national coal miners' strike is affecting the country's industrial production. As a result, the slowdown within the steel industries is impeding the military supply of weaponry.

January 30, 1943
Three months have already passed since I joined the Young Men's Training Group. Under Okubo-san's strict instruction, every day at 10:00 AM the first group of seventeen men and the second group of thirty men practice military drill in the recreation hall. The intense military training has improved my wellbeing and self-control, giving my mind and body a renewed vigour. I am very grateful to Okubo-san for giving us his disciplined instruction.

February 3, 1943
An average of fifteen men from our hut are required to go on work duty every day. Of the seventy-six internees in our hut, some of the men are already on regular kitchen and hospital

crews. Every second or third day, it is my turn to work. According to the kitchen staff, the army has issued them an order to cut down on our food rations. I cannot imagine how they could give us less food. Pretty soon it might be bread and water. The other day we elected Nakagawa-san as our new hut leader. We have received a large amount of notebooks, pencils, and drawing papers from the YMCA.

February 4, 1943

The weather has been fairly mild lately. But today the ice on the windowpanes started getting thicker again as the temperature fell.

I made up my mind with some fellows from the hut to cut my hair short. I walked around the bunkhouse in high spirits, showing off my new crewcut. I feel like I am ten years old again, back in the mischievous days of my early childhood in Japan. We all look awfully different after our haircuts. Everybody looks younger, more childish and playful. We do not really care about the way we look. We laughed at each other's unusual head shapes. Imagawa-kun's head is a *donguri* (acorn) shape as the top part of his head has a high point. Okubo-san's head is like a ski slope, high at the back and sloping down smoothly and straight towards his forehead. Yamamura-kun's head is a lovely lemon shape. They pointed out that my head is also lemon-shaped. Takeda-kun's head, with its squared and dignified head shape, reminds me of a picture I once saw of an old Japanese *nyudo* (a large Buddhist monk). The other men in the hut hushed us and said we were being extremely childish, but we are proud of our short hair and wanted to show it off.

The short hair somehow suits us Japanese men.

There was a church service in the dining hall in the afternoon. Several internees attended the service to hear a white priest give his sermon. He spoke Japanese very well.

February 8, 1943

Lately, I have been thinking about my personality and behaviour. My shyness has always troubled me. Ever since childhood I have been aware of my timid and withdrawn personality.

I believe it has something to do with the circumstances of my upbringing. Living with my aunt's family of cousins, I felt like an orphan. At times I felt I was looked upon as an unwanted family member. I was a shy and quiet boy, always scared to say anything. Even now as a grown man, I still retain some of my fears and inhibitions.

If only I could get rid of my retiring disposition and train myself to be more confident and forward, and not be so afraid to speak in front of others. I would so dearly like to express my own opinions without holding back, and become a lively, bright person just like my good friend Okazaki-kun.

February 15, 1943

Today felt like the coldest part of winter. In spite of the freezing weather, we were still forced to work outside the camp. A snow party was formed and six of us left the camp with a guard to shovel the snow around the railroad tracks. Our feet froze very quickly, as we were only wearing thin cotton socks and summer work boots. In this cold weather, we could not remain outside very long. Eventually, we decided among ourselves to go back to camp and warm up. In the meantime, our guard called the sergeant major in charge of the work crews. The sergeant major came to find us in the recreation hall and demanded that we go back to work but we adamantly refused. We got into a loud argument that resulted in Chiba-kun being sent to the detention house. The sergeant major was evidently satisfied with this, and the snow party was cancelled for the rest of the day. We sat in silence together, agreeing that the animosity between the internees and the army with respect to the forced labour outside in the cold was far from over.

February 16, 1943

We were all surprised to see a small portion of milk, butter and rice as part of the menu today. It has been such a long time since we last saw rice on our tables. We understand that a food shortage is natural on account of the war, but we suspect that the army personnel are redirecting part of our supplies before it reaches the camp. We have no way of proving it.

The food shortage and the forced labour in the cold weather might be part of their strategy to force us to abandon our protest and leave Angler. A visiting official from the government manpower department is always "encouraging" our young men to get out of the camp and get a job outside, so that they can have plenty of good food and good pay for their work. I suppose that twenty-two cents an hour could at least buy some good food.

February 17, 1943

I have so many things on my mind. I would like to learn and

study, but everything is going at such a ponderously slow pace. Lately, I realize that no matter what I am doing during my day, I feel tired. I often feel irritated, and my eyes are sore and become blurry whenever I read. At first I thought that I was the only one, but I later discovered that other internees have the same symptoms.

The exhaustion we are suffering from must be the result of our inadequate diets. We just do not receive enough nourishment. We Japanese need rice in our meals. We only receive rice meals two or three times a month. To top it off, we are hardly eating any fruits or vegetables. It is a shame that even my own determined efforts to keep well cannot counter the effect of being locked up in this icy camp.

JOINED THE YODOKAN JUDO CLUB

February 19, 1943

For some time now I had considered joining the judo club, and first thing this morning, I signed up. Five other men were eager to follow my pursuit.

Our judo *sensei* is a man named Masato Ishibashi-san. He welcomed us into the Yodokan Judo club and praised our decision to learn the art of judo. Judo, he said, would help us improve our inner selves. By the disciplined exercise of mind and body, we can improve our ability to choose what is right and what is wrong. Honest thinking and hard work are right choices for improving the inner self. To hate, quarrel and lie are wrong choices that will eventually lead a man to debauchery. Only with constant practice can a man maintain a friendly, loving disposition while also improving his inner self. His opening words echoed loudly my own sentiments.

Ishibashi-sensei stood before our class of twenty judo participants assembled in the recreation hall and began demonstrating basic *Ukemi*-exercises. By the end of the class we were all well trained on how to fall on the mat. I feel good for having joined the Yodokan Judo Club. It gives me a purpose and reminds me of my own strength. I am proud to have a chance to learn our national sport. I solemnly promise myself to make the best effort to master this martial art.

A Spanish vice-consul visited the camp in the afternoon. He met with the Japanese nationals and discussed at length with Tanaka-san the food shortages, forced labour, medical problems and the relocation of our camp. He made it clear that he has no authority to speak for either the Canadian-born Nisei or the nationalized Canadian citizens, the Kika Issei, who make up a part of our camp. As he left, he gave Tanaka-san over six hundred dollars in donations from the Fairview Woman's Group in Slocan, BC.

February 20, 1943

The severe winter that has locked us in ice for the past three months finally eased into warmer weather today. Our camp was veiled this morning under a thick blanket of fog. We were illuminated by haloed camp lights. The watchtowers peaked through the fog like phantoms.

When the fog lifted around 10:00 AM, it revealed a spectacular scene of tiny ice flowers on the bushes and trees around the camp. I marvelled at the breathtaking view and for a short moment it felt as though I was in a different world. There was no camp, no routine, only a marvellous crystal palace and I was a child in its courtyard.

The afternoon brought more warm weather. All around us the snow began to melt, leaving behind colour that hinted at the warmth to come. Spring is still far away but I can hardly wait for the nice weather.

February 21, 1943

Shortly after breakfast, our Young Men's Training Group gathered in the recreation hall for a training session. We practiced some military drill under the instruction of Okubo-san. From 10:00 AM to noon the judo club members took over. After lunch we held another YMTG study class and at around four the judo club members took over the hall again.

For supper, I ate a tiny portion of dried roast beef with a scoop of mashed potatoes. I placed my empty tray into the wash cart and went back to my bunkhouse. A short time later, I left for my accounting class in the mess hall.

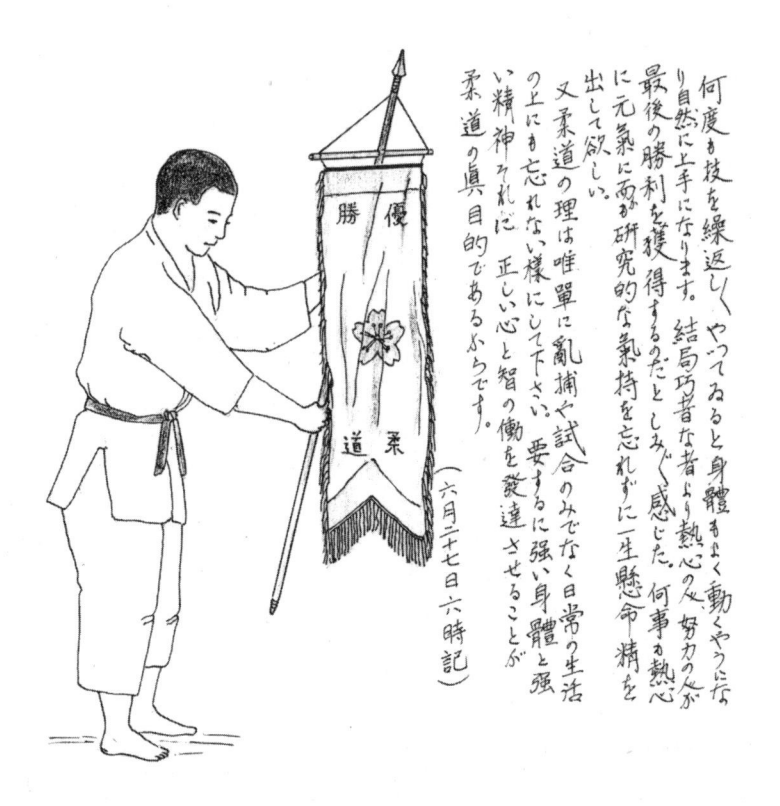

After the evening roll call, I met with a small group of men in the laundry room to practice abdominal respiration. The laundry room is an ideal place for us to practice as the room is located in a quiet area between the two busy huts. Bunjiro Tanaka instructed us on how to expand our abdomen slowly, to fully inhale a breath of air, and then exhale slowly, allowing for the release of our tightly wound muscles. We sat on the floor in the quiet darkness and practiced our deep breathing. I could feel my anxiety slowly fading as I descended into a tranquil state of meditation. After thirty minutes of deep breathing, I felt fully rejuvenated and relaxed, all ready for bed.

Thus I am kept very busy throughout my day. I have very little time to myself. I consider myself fortunate that I can practice the things that I want to while still interned in a prison camp. I might also benefit from a knowledge of music, Japanese handwriting, mathematics, and shorthand writing. All these things I want to do some day.

February 25, 1943:
It was cloudy and cold outside all day. The chilly wind convinced me that winter will keep us cool for a while yet.

I was feeling somewhat uneasy when I had first joined the judo club last week. I am much more comfortable today. I have become better acquainted with most of the members and developed a friendly respect for our instructor Ishibashi-sensei. Before last week, I thought he was a strict and distant man, but my first impressions of him were incorrect. He is a true leader, bright and vivacious in his method and manner. Our club members are greatly influenced by his personality. During our practices, the recreation hall is filled with our enthusiastic, youthful spirit. I very much enjoy being with the judo club every morning.

Regrettably, there is an unfriendly feeling between the Young Men's Training Group (YMTG) and the Judo Club. The members of the YMTG do not have much respect for the Judo Club. They feel that their practices are far superior. I now discover that I was mistaken in previously siding with the YMTG's righteous attitude. I am ashamed when I think back on how the Judo Club accepted me with a respectful, open-minded equality: I was welcomed like a good friend.

We all entered this camp with the same goal of protesting against the government. We should put our minor differences aside and live in unity for the common good.

At 1:00 PM I attended a Judo Club study session in the mess hall. Under Ishibashi-sensei's instruction, we studied some practical movements from judo textbooks. He told us newcomers how judo originated. Then he explained the judo-ka's motto; that the art of judo must only be used in self-defence and was strictly prohibited from being used as a fighting motive. Once we had completed our study, we sang "*Kokyo no haha*" together, then gaily departed. The innocent, cheerful atmosphere lifted my spirits. In these times, we men need a lively and youthful spirit, as well as good mental and physical discipline.

As I stepped out of the classroom, humming "*Kokyo no haha*," the cold wind and snowflakes gently brushed by my cheeks.

February 27, 1943
It snowed off and on all day. Our YMTG members jogged

around the camp for about forty minutes. We regularly run twice a day, in the morning and evening. Once the snow melts, we will be able to run for two hours or even longer.

Horii-kun has been ill for a long time with kidney trouble, and was sent to the hospital in Port Arthur as his condition grew worse. I feel sorry for him, as he is only twenty years old. We have now sadly learned that he is unlikely to recover.

February 29, 1943

I was delightfully surprised to see three eggs on my breakfast plate this morning. We have not had any eggs for such a long time and, all of a sudden, to see three sunny-side eggs made me smile. Our meat supply is still short; though we are now receiving some rice and fish, about twice a week.

March 2, 1943

Today has been the coldest day so far. A guard at the gate told us that the thermometer plunged to almost minus sixty degrees.

At noon, nine men left Angler. They are the first group to be released from the camp this year. More men are certain to depart once the weather warms up. It benefits no one to hold the men back in the camp. If they wanted to depart, the sooner the better. None of us want a reoccurrence of the Petawawa shooting incident, when the army suspected men were trying to escape.

I felt sad when I saw Yoshida-san's face in the crowd of men waiting to depart at the gate. Yoshida-san and I had been together since the beginning of Hastings Park, when we had made our first courageous stand against the government and refused to be taken away to a road camp. That was almost a year ago. Since then, we had shared some difficult times at the Immigration Building, Petawawa, and here in the Angler Concentration Camp. I cannot not help but feel that we are one by one losing our prominent *ganbari ya*.

March 6, 1943

We purchased some apples with the profits from our canteen funds and divided them evenly among the internees. It was quite a treat for us to receive half a dozen apples each, as the supply of fresh fruits is so scarce in this camp.

There was no motion picture showing this Saturday, but some beer was sold at the canteen for twenty cents a bottle.

March 8, 1943

An unsettling rumour was heard in the camp today. The Canadian government is planning to release the internees from Angler and relocate them to a forced-labour camp. A few of the internees are upset by this and fear that it will happen at any time. I heard from some outside news that the US government has already started transferring the American Niseis and naturalized Issei Japanese from their camps and placing them in forced-labour camps. I assume that the Canadian government will naturally soon follow.

March 11, 1943

We received a notice from the camp commander today. All internees must be assembled outside for physical exercise from 10:00 AM to 11:00 AM, and 2:00 PM to 3:00 PM, weather permitting. Anyone caught indoors during these hours will be sent to do forced labour or sent to the detention house.

The detention house is a small building located near the camp gate. It has two window slits near the top and four bunk beds set along the walls. Most of the men sent to the detention house are confined there after arguing with the guards while on an outside working crew. Otherwise, the detention house is usually vacant, as there is seldom any trouble with the internees in the camp.

Many internees became infuriated when they heard the notice to assemble outside for exercise during the appointed hours. They protested that we did our own exercise of our own free spirit and the army had no right to dictate when, how, where or how long we would exercise. If the army is so worried about our health, they should give us better food rations.

March 13, 1943

We received an overseas announcement from Japan today that was intercepted by a short-wave radio somewhere in the ghost town area. At 6:00 PM, on March 9, 1943, a Japanese declaration was announced at the public meeting hall in Kanda, Tokyo. Ministers Hachiro Arita and Tsurukichi Murayama, and General Kichizaburo Nomura delivered a speech in front of over five thousand Japanese people. It was later broadcast countrywide and overseas.

Based on several reports from people returning to Japan, they are greatly concerned about the safety of Japanese countrymen living abroad in enemy countries. They are very proud of these countrymen, devoting their lives to developing ties and founding a binding unity between Japan and foreign countries.

As a show of respect for these overseas countrymen, they declared that they will make their best effort to provide overseas countrymen with fresh Japanese supplies. They encouraged the overseas countrymen to continue with their support and be confident that the Japanese Empire is making every effort to end the war.

March 14, 1943

Two high-ranking officials from Ottawa visited the camp today. They performed a routine inspection of the camp. Our spokesman Tanaka-san met with them and requested that they investigate the amount of supplies being given to the internees. He expressed his concern that the health of the internees is getting worse as they are not receiving a sufficient amount of food.

March 15, 1943

I have been practicing abdominal respiration every night now for the past two months. I feel that I may still not be practicing the technique properly, as I have had little evidence of any benefit. Bunjiro Tanaka-san has practiced this technique for many years, and I think that I could learn more from him if he instructed me in private. I thought of asking him, and shared my intention with the Judo Club. We discussed my idea and decided that it would benefit all of us if we were given added instruction as a group. Tanaka-san began giving us further instruction the following evening.

The Mass Evacuation Movement Group disbanded today. They announced that all members of the MEM Group are free to make their own decisions regarding their individual welfare.

March 20, 1943:

On account of the rapid change in the weather lately, colds are spreading among the internees. Fourteen men from our hut have been admitted to the infirmary with high fevers. This is a sure sign of influenza.

March 21, 1943

We have been informed that Horii-kun, who was admitted to the Port Arthur hospital on February 27 with a kidney infection, sadly passed away at the hospital on March 8. We held a memorial service for Horii-kun at the recreation hall, to pray for his young soul, gone at the age of twenty.

March 26, 1943

Today was my turn to be on the work crew. Four of us were assigned to clean the army barracks, dining room, and kitchen. The savoury smell of baked fish coming from the iron stoves clutched at my empty stomach. As we completed our work, we joked about having to clean up after the army.

We were taking a short break when a two-striped guard entered the kitchen and angrily criticized us for being idle. Without a moment's thought, he immediately confined us to the detention house.

We prepared a response in the event that there was a hearing on the matter. At 2:00 PM, a sergeant major came in and told us to go back to work until 4:00 PM and no charges would be laid. Our plan was to remain in the detention house until we were given a chance to explain ourselves. We felt somewhat insulted by the guard's rashness. We were persuaded to return to work when Tanaka-san visited us and explained that he would address the matter with the camp commander.

March 28, 1943

The severe influenza that has afflicted many internees over the past two months is showing signs of weakening. Men are slowly returning from the infirmary and the empty beds in our hut have started to fill up again. I am fortunate that I did not become sick. My body must have been made strong inside.

April 1, 1943

For the first time in almost six months, the thermometer climbed above the freezing mark yesterday. At last the long bitter winter is almost at an end. Spring has finally returned to Angler. The snow on the ground has started to melt, exposing some bare brown turf here and there. After being cooped up for five long months, it is so nice to finally see the snow melting and to be able to take a fresh breath from the warm humid breeze.

After lunching on soup and sandwiches, I went back to the bunkhouse and persuaded Hirakawa-kun and Maehara-san to come outside for a walk on the grounds. It is too nice a day to be sitting idle inside. M. Gune Kawahira-kun has been my close friend since Petawawa. Gune-chan is around my age. He was wearing oversized boots that made a big slapping noise when he walked. Everyone adores his good-natured personality. Always pleasant and direct, never angry or argumentative with anyone. I enjoy speaking with him, his artless Kagoshima-dialect relaxes me and I am always able to speak clearly about what is on my mind.

Maehara-san is in his fifties, which makes him one of the oldest internees in Angler. He had lived in Mission, BC as a market gardener before the war. In late 1920, his father purchased fifty acres of uncultivated land, and together they made a beautiful farm that produced strawberries, corn, cucumber, and other vegetables. He often showed me his family pictures and told me about his farm life while in the verdant Fraser Valley.

His wife and two daughters are now living in the Lemon Creek relocation centre in the interior of BC. In early 1942, shortly after the war between Japan and Canada began, Maehara-san received an eviction notice delivered by an RCMP officer who demanded that he vacate his property immediately. He refused to leave and remained behind when his wife and two daughters tearfully boarded a wagon with their few possessions. The RCMP later removed Maehara-san by force.

Most of the time he stayed inside the bunkhouse playing cards or just lying on his bed with his hands resting behind his head. I was happy to see him outside in the sun. Gune-chan and I walked back along the barbed wire fence to where he had stopped.

We paused for a moment by his side and together looked out towards the nearby hills, then cheerfully encouraged him to continue with us on our walk.

April 3, 1943

Today we were required by the army to exchange our old canteen coupons for new ones. My brother and I had spent twenty dollars since being interned. We each had another thirty dollars remaining. After talking about what we had purchased and what we really needed, we thought it best to only spend ten dollars each per year. Our budget would allow our money to last for another three years.

April 4, 1943

We were now able to do some of our Young Men's Training exercises outside, as most of the snow on the ground had melted.

In the evening, we heard thunder for the first time in six months and then it started to rain. The little snow remaining would be gone by morning.

April 6, 1943

The Wartime Prices and Trade Board has devised a rationing regulation that comes into effect this month. The nationwide moderation scheme was instituted to protect the diminishing supply of household goods needed by Canadians during wartime.

We have been given a list of restrictions on the supplies that can be purchased from the canteen. The restrictions have very little effect on us, as we have never been permitted to purchase anything close to the listed amounts. The following is an outline of the restrictions on the goods we can purchase:

50 cigarettes per week
1 bar of soap per 3 weeks
1 cigarette holder per year
2 notebooks per year
100 cigarette papers per week
2 boxes of phonograph needles per month
12 cigarette lighters per year

4 phonograph records per month

1/4 pound of tobacco per week

3 fountain pens per year

1 pack of cards per year

1 package of gum per week

1 chocolate bar per week

1/2 dozen handkerchiefs per year

1/4 pound of biscuits per week

1 pair of cloth slippers per year

2 face towels per year

1 jar of face cream per year

2 bath towels per year

1 small mirror per year

4 tubes of toothpaste per year

The restrictions on these items apply to the internees in the camp, but an army authority informed us that, as a result of the war, the restrictions will also apply to all Canadians.

April 11, 1943
The cool weather has continued for several days. Mr. Phypher, a representative from the manpower department, was here again from Ottawa to encourage internees wishing to submit their applications for a release to work camps. Over one hundred internees met with him at the gate.

The way things are going, Angler is bound to end up half empty by summer. The only men remaining in the camp will be those from the Citizenship Renouncement Group, judo members, older Isseis and *ganbari ya* such as myself.

A LONG-AWAITED SPRING

April 19, 1943

At last, the long cruel winter that dominated us for five long months has finally come to an end. The morning breeze is still cool, but the soft ground beneath my feet and the blue sky above fill me with a great joy for the oncoming spring. The cries of distant seagulls wafted by the warm morning air brushed away my winter gloom and left me feeling rejuvenated. Spring is in bloom. I felt happy and began to sing *"sora wa aozora,"* the sky is blue and we are young.

At 8:00 PM the sound of a trumpet signalled our evening roll call. We lined up outside for the first time since last autumn. The setting sun tinted the hilltops with an orange hue as the eastern sky began changing to a pale grey. A lone seagull circled overhead as we waited for the sergeant major's command. I looked at the men around me. How refreshed their faces looked after the end of their long

hibernation. "Six paces forward," broke the still moment and the sound of our footsteps echoed sharply on the whitewashed walls. I was vividly reminded of our last outdoor roll call.

A lonely sky above at the evening roll call,
A lone seagull is flying back to the Great Lakes,
With a setting sun reflected on its silver wings.

Tenko suru kurezora sabishi kamomera no,
Shiroi tsubasa ni yuhi kagayaku.

April 21, 1943

The fine weather continues. The ground is getting dry enough for men to start playing ball. I remarked how wonderful it is to smell the sweet spring air again. I sat at leisure outside, taking some notes while watching the internees play baseball.

We received 150 pounds of Japanese tea, delivered to us by the last exchange ship.

April 27, 1943

Dr. Hori was released from the camp today. We are going to miss him, as he was the only doctor in Angler. Now we will be at the complete mercy of the army's bush doctors.

Some twenty men met with Mr. Phypher, who was here again today to promote work outside.

May 4, 1943

The sky has been cloudy for the last couple of days. I am glad to see the morning sun bright in the sky, warming us nicely with spring-like weather. I can see that the snow on the distant mountains is melting and the tamarack trees are budding nicely around the camp. I feel very much alive.

We have received another $150 donation from the Catholic Church Society.

May 10, 1943

After two months of training on the judo *ukemi* technique of how to fall without injury, we have begun practicing a basic foot trick called *ashi waza*. We put some old canvas-covered army mattresses on the floor, but the limited amount of mattresses only permitted a very narrow area to practice on. There are five other men besides Ishibashi-sensei who held black belts in judo. Our club is growing larger every day with the enrolment of newcomers. We have decided to split our club into morning and evening groups, to free up some space on the *judoba* floor.

My back is sunburned from working outside in the hot sun today. We are busy preparing for the upcoming Navy Day celebration. A sumo-wrestling match will be one of the main attractions for the day. We have constructed a *dohyo ba*, a wrestling ring, by levelling and packing down an area of sandy ground, and chalking a white border around it. When it was completed, a few of the men shouted with some excitement that they wanted to try it out. I was still busy stamping the sand near the edges when I was abruptly pulled into the ring. I threw myself into the fray. When the fun was all over, I walked back to my hut with Gune-chan, laughing, all covered with sand from head to toe.

After supper we assembled in the recreation hall and held a memorial service for the late Chozo Takahashi, who passed away a year ago at the Winnipeg hospital on his way to the Petawawa concentration camp. Reverend Mitsubayashi began with a Buddhist sutra-chant followed by a condolence speech from Tanaka-san.

May 27, 1943

Today was Navy Day in Japan. All the internees gathered on the fog-covered grounds before the morning roll call and made a respectful *yohai* salute towards the east. On account of bad weather, our planned sumo-wrestling event has been cancelled until next Sunday.

May 28, 1943

It was my turn to be on a work crew today. Small birds chirped playfully in the surrounding trees. Yellow dandelions and purple violets bloomed heartily on the roadside just outside the gate and served to accent the beauty of this day.

Last year, there was always at least one guard to escort every five internees while outside the camp. Now there is only one guard for the ten of us. They have realized that there is no need to worry, as we are unlikely to make an attempt to escape. As long as there is no superior around, the guards treat us with a casual lenience.

The guard with us today is named Joe. He says he is from Nova Scotia. Once we had completed our job of emptying garbage into a pit, we asked Joe if we could go on a hike. The good-natured guard said it was okay as long as we were back in time for lunch. We dragged him around the hills and bushes near the railroad for a good hour. It was wonderful to enjoy some freedom outside, laughing under the spring sun.

The fresh air outside Angler seems much different from the stale air inside. I breathed in the spring air and delighted in the sweet smell of flowers and green grass. I looked down from the hill we had climbed and peered at the grandness of Lake Superior. I listened to the silvery cries of the seagulls flying lazily over the lakeshore below. I revelled in the abundant glory of spring.

It does not matter where I am, I have always liked spring-time the best. In rainy Skeena River, my native place, or in snow-bound Echigo, northern Japan, where I grew up, I always awaited the arrival of spring with great anticipation. Even in this lonely, solitary corner of the world, spring has arrived and brought me a renewed joy for life. Nature provides a refreshing warmth. Its kind hands cradle every living thing on Earth with complete fairness and equality.

May 29, 1943

We inquired about the sudden shortage of food rations we had been receiving lately. The army authorities gave us a nonchalant answer, saying that they were trying to even out our rations after mistakenly giving us too much. They must have thought we were nothing more than cats and dogs.

May 30, 1943

Our scheduled sumo-wrestling activity was cancelled again on account of the bad weather. All day a strong wind blew across the nearby fields, raising a cloud of sand high up in the air.

After supper we held an evening of entertainment in the recreation hall and treated ourselves to some apples and ice cream. We forgot about our group differences and enjoyed a friendly evening together.

June 1, 1943

A Spanish Consul visited us again today. Tanaka-san and some Isseis met with him in the afternoon. Tanaka-san made some requests regarding the improvement of our infirmary, and asked if a receiver radio could be placed in our huts. He requested that the camp be relocated to a warmer climate. He inquired about the possibility of exchanging prisoners, as some Isseis want to go back to Japan. He informed the Consul about the army's idea of balancing out our food rations. He inquired about the mail service delay and the forced labour regulation within the army compound.

June 8, 1943

Ten men were released from the camp today. A commotion arose when an army authority seized some notes from one of the departing men. The notes included a report describing the nature of the Canadian government and the army's deportment regarding the Petawawa shooting incident. It also reported the case of the late Horii-kun, who died from improper treatment. We received a strict notice from the camp commander that the person responsible for this document will be immediately confined to the detention house for twenty-eight days and later be sent to a military tribunal.

June 13, 1943

The leaves on the trees surrounding the camp are growing more vibrant by the day. A warm southerly wind brings me the assurance that summer is coming.

Our Yodokan Judo Club held an exhibition this afternoon. Ban-kun began the event by demonstrating his free-style judo *waza* against eleven men in succession. He is a first-dan black belt, standing five and a half feet tall and weighing no more than 130 pounds.

After formally bowing before his first opponent, Ban-kun quickly caught and twisted him over his hip, then threw him

firmly onto the mat. Once he was thrown onto the mat, it was a decided match for one point. His second opponent took a moment longer to get hold of but was finally caught off guard and thrown over his shoulder onto the mat. The third man who challenged him was T. Marubashi, a bigger man. Ban-kun waited for him then stepped aside, tripping him onto the mat and then pinning him down. His fourth and fifth opponents were also quickly thrown onto the mat. The sixth opponent almost pinned Ban-kun, but he managed to turn swiftly on the mat and pin him down instead. The seventh, eight and ninth opponents all tried different *waza* tactics but were easily pinned down. The tenth opponent tried to throw Ban-kun out but was thrown over his shoulder and onto the mat. The eleventh man charged for Ban-kun and was flipped over his shoulder and onto the mat. It was simply breathtaking. Everyone applauded the performance. We commenced our tournament with a renewed enthusiasm. I made a nice throw on my first opponent but lost on the second match.

After supper our Judo Club assembled in the mess hall and sat together for a tea party to express our gratitude towards Ishibashi-sensei and the other black belts for their devoted efforts in teaching us.

June 27, 1943

Today we held a judo tournament to determine grade advancement. I ended the day with one win, two losses and two ties. I had fought well, considering I only knew two or three moves. Four months have passed already since I first joined the Judo Club. I feel good and am satisfied with my progress.

July 5, 1943

Three representatives from each hut met in the mess hall with Suzuki-san, Kamishiro-san, and Akiyama-san. The three internees are scheduled to return to Japan on the next exchange ship. A few points about the living conditions in the Angler concentration camp were brought to their attention in the hope that they will report the details back to the Japanese government.

July 7, 1943

Another twenty-two men were released from the camp today. Five of them were from my hut. About nine months ago, over 760 internees occupied this camp. Now only about five hundred internees remain. At one time our hut seemed crowded, with almost eighty internees living there. Now many of the bunks are empty, making our hut seem large and empty.

July 11, 1943

We held an athletic exhibition today to celebrate the sixth anniversary of the China Armed Conflict. Six years ago, Japan went to war with China. It was a perfect day for the event, as the sky cleared nicely once the morning fog lifted. It was an exciting day for all the internees, as men from their respective huts were to compete against each other in all kinds of athletic games.

At 10:00 AM the selected teams began marching the grounds with their hut-numbered flags at the forefront—2-A, 2-B, 3-A, 3-B, 4-A, 4-B, 5-A, 5-B. The Angler band played in the style of an *aikoku koshin kyoku*, popular Japanese band, and all the men marched in high spirits, as though they were marching straight into the Olympic games. Tanaka-san gave an excellent opening speech that was followed by a description of the day's program by the Kotera sports and entertainment director.

The gigantic Angler summer games were underway. The Judo Club and the YMTG club members set themselves to the task of refereeing and assisting. There was a three-legged race, a one-hundred-metre, two-hundred-metre, and four-hundred-metre spoon race, and an obstacle-course race. Men carried fifty-pound sandbags, laughing and straining while they raced for the finish line. There was a horse carriage race, consisting of three men shoulder to shoulder pretending to be the horse team and one man on top as the driver. One event had men placing gunnysacks over their heads and bobbling blindly to the sounds of the cheering crowd on the sideline. There were father-and-son team races, a twelve-hundred-metre elderly relay race, and a twelve-hundred-metre youth relay race. The games lasted until suppertime.

Everyone was out cheering and having fun under the sun. Huts 5-A and 5-B ended the day with a tie, both having won an equal majority of points in the events. Upon closing the games, Tanaka-san waited a few moments before our crowd quieted down, then delivered a great speech that congratulated everyone who had participated in the games.

Today was the most enjoyable day for us since having been interned. It was so good to see all the internees having fun together, forgetting their opinions, identities and differences. All of us enjoyed a friendly, fun-filled day together.

July 12, 1943
As a follow-up to yesterday's event, we held a tug-of-war com-

petition. We selected the twenty strongest men from our hut and set out to compete against our rival 5-B hut. Our team members were on average smaller then the other team members, yet our team had a united strength and a superior morale. After many prolonged grunts and strained shouts, our team pulled all of the opposing team members from the 5-B hut well over the chalked line. With a great cheer, our hut members hailed us as the true Angler champions.

The Kotera sports and entertainment director proclaimed us the most athletic men in the camp and, after some applause, gave our hut leader Nakagawa-san twenty dollars' worth of prize money in the form of canteen coupons.

August 3, 1943

Summer has finally arrived to Angler, but it is already like fall outside, as a cool wind blows briskly from the north.

Eight men left the camp today. My good friend K-san was among them.

August 10, 1943

Six more internees have been released from the camp. The empty beds in the huts increase every day as more and more men leave. Some of the *ganbari ya* called them cowards.

As for myself, I miss them and recall all the good and bad times we shared together. Their parting is especially painful, as some of them had been close to me since the time of the Immigration Building in Vancouver. I could not hold back my tears when I saw them depart. I silently pray for their good health.

August 11, 1943

It is the middle of summer and the daytime temperature in Angler remains cool. The climate here is very different from Petawawa, where we experienced an unbearably hot summer.

Half a year has already passed since I joined the Judo Club. During that time, I have learned five *tachi wazas*, tricks in the standing position; four *newaza*, moves and holds in the laying position; and four chokeholds. I am gaining more confidence. In such a short time, I have learned a higher self-control and greatly increased my mental and physical strength. I am very

雄々しく闘つた選士達は今静かに午前の戦跡を
追憶してゐるのであらう。採點表を圍んでゐるもの
ニッコリと面上に笑みをたべて道場を去つて行く後姿
もある。午后の策戦を錬る者も居る。取へて
云ふ。若友よ平常の心になれと。

grateful to Ishibashi-sensei and all the black belts and senior club members for having shared their knowledge.

I am dedicating more time lately to learning English. I learned some English while in Japan, but forgot most of it after leaving school, living and working as I did with Japanese people who only spoke Japanese. Some of the men around me believe that there will be no use for English once Japan has won the war. I believe that the English language is still worth studying regardless of what nation wins the war.

The internees have a tendency to get restless when they have free time and nothing to do. Eventually they develop negative and undesirable thoughts, and become noticeably dissatisfied. Bearing this in mind, I remind myself to make an added effort to keep myself occupied at all times.

August 15, 1943

It was clear in the morning. By noon the blue sky was completely covered by a thick blanket of low clouds that had rolled in from the nearby lakes. The cool humid air feels very much like autumn. Only a pale light penetrates the mist, casting an early veil of darkness over our barracks as the evening roll call approached.

I placed my pencil and paper aside and lay down on my bed. There was not enough light to continue with the drawings that I wanted to complete by this afternoon. As I lay there, my thoughts went back to my childhood days at an Obon festival in the Japanese countryside. Dressed in my new kimono and wearing a pair of wooden shoes, I had joined a circle of Obon dancers. The evening was warm and romantic. We danced together under the twilight stars, with the light of the fire filling our thoughts. I can still hear the simple folk song and feel the steady, heart-pounding beat of the Taiko drums. As I fell asleep, I felt like a child, and dreamt of a time that was so tender and carefree.

August 18, 1943

I volunteered to help in the kitchen, as the cooking crew was short-staffed today. We prepared food for over five hundred internees. The kitchen is a very large place, with two rows of large, coal-burning stoves surrounded by dozens of over-sized pots and pans. More cooks arrived around lunchtime, and the place grew very hot and boisterous with men busily preparing meals on the many burning stoves.

August 24, 1943

Suzuki-san, Kamishiro-san and Akiyama-san were given notice of their departure some time today. It seems like a sure thing this time. They will make the long trip back to Japan with the exchange ship that arrives in New York around mid-October. All of the Japanese in North America who are repatriating to Japan are scheduled to assemble and wait for the exchange ship in New York. The ship will carry them from the east coast of the United States across the Atlantic Ocean to the southern tip of Africa, then up through the Indian Ocean, through the archipelagos of the Philippines and then finally to Japan.

There was a crowd at the gate to see them off. These three men had been the first internees to arrive at the Petawawa concentration camp in early 1942. They could not hide their joy at finally leaving the camp. They made their farewell handshakes and said their solemn goodbyes then walked happily through the gate. I saw them turn around two or three times to glance back at the barbed wire fences and the familiar encampment that had been their home for so long. I watched their figures recede in the distance and prayed for their safe voyage to Japan.

Since being interned over a year ago, I have become closely acquainted with Akiyama-san. We occupied different bunkhouses but I often met with him. He never talked about what he had done before the war, but I could tell that he was an educated man. We spoke about many interesting things. I was impressed by his keen understanding of the world around him. He told me many times, like my father, "Study hard, for now you are given the chance."

The train's whistle echoed through the hills, sounding the men's departure to Japan and perhaps blessing them with a clear and final goodbye.

August 25, 1943

Another twenty men have been released from the camp. They were going to work in bush camps, cutting pulpwood in Schriber, Neis and Nipigan, Ontario, near the north shore of Lake Superior.

Our manufactured Kendo uniforms finally arrived from the Ghost Town relocation centre today. Matsushita-san, a fourth-dan black belt in the art of Kendo, will be the sensei to the forty men who joined the new club.

Whenever I sparred with Matsushita-san in the *judoba*, I felt that he was a dangerous man. His piercing eyes seemed to bore right through me. Once I got to know him, I realized that he was a kind man—very enthusiastic and correct in his manner. I could hardly wait to learn the art of Kendo.

September 4, 1943

We received a notice from the camp commander that huts 5-A and 5-B will be closed due to the diminishing number of occupants within the two huts. We must move to another hut.

After the evening roll call we held a farewell party for our hut-mates who had bunked together for over a year. There were forty-four of us gathered around the tables set in the centre of our bunkhouse.

Our hut vice-leader Nishimura-san, recited a brief farewell speech in place of our hut leader, Nakagawa-san, who had taken sick and was now nursing a flu in the infirmary. We enjoyed an evening of camaraderie, chewing biscuits and sipping tea while reminiscing about the friendly times we had shared in our hut. We tarried until 10:30 PM and then sauntered off to bed.

September 5, 1943

We began moving into the neighbouring hut soon after the morning roll call. It was already lunch by the time I had completely moved into hut number 3-A along with the twenty-two other men. I found an empty bunk by the stove, near the east side of the bunkhouse, and placed my belongings on a nearby shelf.

After evening roll call, our new hut leader Hayashi-san gave us our chores list and laundry schedule. He then gave us an important notice from the camp commander. There is a national shortage of coal due to the ongoing war efforts and the commander wants some internees to volunteer for a wood-cutting crew. He fears that the camp might be unable to make it through the cold winter months with its depleted stockpile of coal. The volunteers will be paid twenty cents a day.

September 6, 1943

I am somewhat uncomfortable in my new hut. There are seventy-four men in our bunkhouse, many more than were in my old hut. I know that it will take some time to get used to the new faces around me, but still I find it difficult. I overheard someone saying that our hut houses the youngest internees in Angler. I had already met most of the men in the camp at some time during our internment together. They are not complete strangers to me, but I still know only half their names. I remind myself to be patient.

September 10, 1943

The temperature plummeted when a terrible storm passed through our camp the other day. A cover of frost on the ground surprised me this morning. Although it is still early September, some of the leaves on the trees are already changing colour. Winter's shallow breath is not far away.

Most of the wildflowers near the barbed wire fence have disappeared. Only a few daisies remain standing in the distant fields. These small white flowers stay in bloom the longest and seem to prevail even in this harsh environment. They give my lonely heart inspiration and hope. Soon they too will depart, one by one, leaving an empty field, just as my friends who will soon leave Angler.

September 15, 1943

A gusty wind blows across the fields, and a lone seagull flaps its white wings in the pale sky, swept away by the high, gusting wind.

Four men left the camp today. One of them was our judo instructor Kawaguchi-san. From the beginning, Kawaguchi ni-dan had been a brilliant assistant for our instructor Ishibashi-san. He had made a great effort and displayed much ability helping our beginners. His departure will be a great loss to our Judo Club.

September 20, 1943

The frost-covered camp and surrounding fields reflected brightly under the clear sky this morning. I was fully awakened by the brisk air that chilled me on my walk to the dining hall.

Our hut leaders met today to discuss the camp commander's request for volunteers. They began by reminding us of our situation in Angler. We have lost our families, homes, and possessions. We have demonstrated our opinions towards the government's actions and been forcibly interned.

Many of us in Angler believe that even though we have lost everything, we still retain our rights as Canadian citizens. We feel violated by the government's actions and do not intend to comply with the government's demands. We are determined to remain in Angler until the government recognizes our rights. We believe that the more we demonstrate our opposition, the more likely it is that the government will realize that we are justified in standing up for our rights.

The hut leaders voted unanimously against the idea of having men volunteer to cut firewood. Tanaka-san submitted a note to the camp commander stating our disapproval of the idea and ultimate refusal to co-operate.

September 21, 1943

My brother Shig and I received a letter from our parents today. My father wrote that they are surviving well and encouraged me to study and train hard for the future to come. It was an encouraging letter, and tenderly reminded me of all the good times we spent together as a family in Skeena River.

September 28, 1943

A secretary of the Spanish Consulate arrived at our camp this afternoon. In the past, an army official always accompanied Tanaka-san, but on this occasion he was able to speak with him in private. Perhaps the new camp commander is showing us some favour to make himself seem more reputable, or perhaps he is showing us a new respect.

The secretary informed Tanaka-san that our request to relocate the camp is out of the question, as there is no evidence of serious illness or detrimental effects posed to the internees by the climate.

Tanaka-san asked if anything was being done about the insufficient amount of relief funds our families are receiving in the BC relocation area. He made a request for some medicine to be supplied to our dilapidated infirmary. He also asked for an inquiry into our food rations, a receiver radio so we can hear the news, and that some commemorative photographs be taken of the internees.

September 29, 1943

A sudden visit from Major General Alexander, a chief commissioner of the Internment Operation Department, sent the army into a reeling panic today. All of us were in a rush to tidy up the kitchen and bunkhouses while some army personnel hurriedly transferred medical supplies and food rations from their compound into our camp. The old, gentle-faced general's inspection was very brief and he departed after only a short time.

October 3, 1943

This morning's beautiful cobalt sky promises us fine autumn weather. My brother Shig and I, along with a few other internees, joined the new kendo club today. I am a member of all three clubs in Angler: kendo, judo, and YMTG. My daily schedule is very busy. Combined with my other academic studies, I am left with very little free time.

October 5, 1943

It seems to me that the scenery around the camp has changed to autumn colours before my very eyes. We received a visitor from Ottawa this morning. His name was D.C. Saul, a register general for enemy aliens. He met with our spokesman, Tanaka-san, and asked if he knows the intentions of the internees, if they are willing to remain or want to leave the camp. Tanaka-san confessed that he did not know the intentions of the internees.

A cold north wind whips through the trees surrounding the camp. The cruel winter will soon arrive to bury the fallen leaves under its sheet of icy snow.

Two more men were released from the camp today. One of

them was a member of our judo club. He was teary eyed this morning when he met our club to say goodbye. He informed us that he hoped to be reunited with his parents in Montreal.

The evening judo class set aside for newcomers commenced today. This will allow the experienced judo participants more room to practice during the day. Some of us judo members who took part in the day class met together while Ishibashi instructed the evening class. We met outside and discussed the idea of creating a commemorative book for Ishibashi-sensei. It will be a token of our gratitude for his tremendous efforts and achievements as head of the Angler Yodokan Judo Club. I was asked to sketch some portraits for the book.

October 14, 1943

The north wind brought us a freezing cold rain all morning. By evening the rain had changed to sleet. The short autumn seems to have passed by so quickly.

> A chilly autumn wind blows on the lonely hillside
> Where the wild daisies have disappeared.
> Sleet-covered trees stand
> Lonely in the evening sky,
> Another day has passed by in
> This strange land.

> *Sabishisa wa itsutomo wakanu*
> *Susonobe ni,*
> *Shiragiku chirite akikaze zo fuku.*
> *Mizore furu kareki sabishiya yumagure,*
> *Kyomo kureruka ekyo no sora ni.*

THE FIRST SNOW

October 17, 1943

It began snowing in the early morning hours. By the time I had dressed and walked to breakfast the camp was completely covered in a gentle white coverlet.

October 20, 1943

The sky was clear this morning after letting fall a foot of snow overnight. I thought it would be really cold as I looked out from my icy window. Once outside, I went for a quick run around the camp and was warmed up nicely and feeling quite refreshed.

The sun appeared in the eastern sky and cast a beautiful golden reflection on the snow-capped mountains and the tops of the watchtowers. Looking up at the cobalt sky, I saw a pale crescent moon floating in the air like a half-eaten bean cake. The snow began melting in the afternoon and some bare ground showed here and there.

I sat at my table gazing out of the warm sunny window at the snowy scenery outside and was reminded of early March, in Ichigo, Japan. For a while my mind went back to my innocent childhood days. Having found a dry patch in the melting snow, my friends and I played with marbles until the older boys returned from the general store, bringing back some candy and a surprise photograph. All of us excitedly climbed atop a dry tin roof and watched as the darkened negative began to develop under the warm afternoon sun. Pressed around the photograph for a better view, we all delighted as the familiar cartoon pictures and faces slowly began to appear.

Feelings of anxiety and uneasiness soon crept up on me as I sat in that stale place. If I let my guard down, the gruelling monotony of the camp makes me feel restless. I resolve once again to keep myself busy both mentally and physically so there can be no time for boredom or depression.

October 21, 1943

The golden sun continued to shine upon us all day. The wet snow on the ground has almost completely melted away.

A government official from the Enemy Aliens Registry Department visited the camp again this morning. As usual, the purpose of his visit was to publicize the work camps and encourage the internees to leave Angler.

October 23, 1943

Before the war, Canada was known as one of the greatest coal-producing nations in the world. But fuel demands for the war efforts are constantly increasing, and the frequent coal-miners' strikes are greatly slowing production. These factors have contributed to the severe national coal shortage that is affecting all areas of the country. The winter months are fast approaching and we have only received two freight cars of coal. It is sur-

prising that we have not been given any further notice concerning the cutting of firewood.

October 26, 1943
The other day I volunteered as a kitchen stoker. Getting up at 5:00 AM was work in itself, but it got easier as the day pro-

gressed. The stoker's job is very hot and dirty; nobody likes this job. There are six large coal-burning stoves set in the centre of the kitchen. I was required to feed the coals into the stoves, take the ashes out, and ensure that the stoves are releasing sufficient heat for the cooks.

Burning the lower-grade coal requires some skill and effort. It gives off good heat as long as it is well tended. The coal does not leave any ashes once it has completely burned. It forms lava-like cinders that become cemented to the bottom of the stoves instead. If too much cinder is allowed to accumulate, the air passages become clogged and the stove extinguishes completely. It is fiery work, to be constantly scraping and prodding through the burning coals to clear out the cinders.

I eventually became more interested in this hot and dirty work. I observed how the coals burned within the stove and carefully piled them so they could burn evenly and allow for the best heat to be produced. At the end of the day, all the cooks praised me as an excellent fireman. I felt very pleased with myself. A job well done. In the future, I might do demanding or disagreeable work and find myself unhappy with my labours. But if I pay attention to the work and give myself a chance to enjoy it, I might find it easier and become more successful at doing the job.

I should try with my utmost ability to master the necessary skills for whatever I do in life. A person who is an expert growing vegetables in the garden, by virtue of his work ethic, may also become an excellent carpenter or blacksmith. As long as he devotes himself to his work, he will accomplish his task with the highest degree of success.

October 27, 1943

The fine weather continues. There is not a cloud in the sky. The wind is a little on the chilly side, but the warm sunrays shine through our bunkhouse windows making it feel like spring.

We have received a notice from the camp commander. It states that arguments with the guards are strictly forbidden while on work duty outside the camp. Our differences should be noted and brought to the attention of the camp leader upon returning to the camp. The camp leader will then present the problem to the camp commander and the matter will be dealt with at the time.

It sounds very reasonable. But it is an altogether different proposal when we are stuck in a dark and filthy coal-car, unloading coal all day. We need to breathe some air once in a while and escape the dust. The guards hardly allow us to catch our breath before they force us back inside at gunpoint.

November 3, 1943

As November rolls in, the warm Indian summer retreats. A cold northerly wind chills the camp with icy snowflakes.

We celebrated the second *Meiji Setsu* in Angler. All the internees gathered in the recreation hall at 9:00 AM to celebrate the Meiji Emperor's birthday. Ironically, this may be the only place in all of Canada that would permit this kind of public ceremony.

November 6, 1943

The cold snowy days continue.

According to a few news reports, the country-wide coal

miner strike is growing worse in the US and Canada. There are fifty-three thousand strikers in the US and about nine thousand in Canada. Americans and Canadians are threatened by a severe fuel shortage that will almost certainly have an adverse affect on transportation and housing. The threat is being passed down to our camp. The firewood-cutting subject was addressed again, but twenty cents a day is little incentive for us to become servants for the camp officials.

November 7, 1943

We held an entertainment event in the recreation hall as an extended holiday to the *Meiji Setsu*. The hall was crowded with internees, glad to be inside and warm. We enjoyed a hearty afternoon, entertained by an old traditional Namiwabushi storyteller, some Japanese folk-singers and several dancers. We treated ourselves with some apples that we had purchased with our canteen funds. Later, some of us played *Shogi*.

We were very appreciative of the entertainment and social

organizer, Kotera-san, who tried so very hard to bring cheer to the men interned within the dreary camp.

November 8, 1943

I submitted a letter to Yushikuni today, of my impressions of the Yodokan Judo Club. He smiled when he read it and informed me that he would place it within our commemorative book.

I wrote:

> I had never dreamed of learning judo before the war. It was a great opportunity that I was given. My days were filled with joy and excitement whenever I practised in the *judoba*. Although I was restrained behind the fences, I was always energetically free. Even in the cold winter days, my inner self was warm and flowing like a spring wind. I was grateful that my days were filled with the aspirations to improve myself. I was grateful for having a means to express myself. I will honour my gratitude by training myself so that someday I can master the art of judo.

November 9, 1943

A swirling north wind descended from Hudson Bay and brought in some heavy snow overnight. By morning the camp was transformed into a white canvas. It is almost impossible to distinguish the ground from the buildings blanketed in the heavy snow.

Dr. Marg visited us again today. He said he had just arrived from an inspection tour of the Japanese Canadian Ghost Towns relocation area in British Columbia, as requested by the Japanese government. He had nothing more to say about his findings. He is here to ensure that we have received the distrib-

ution of *shoyu, miso,* magazines and other recreational goods
that were shipped from Japan some time ago.

November 11, 1943

A pressing matter has been looming over the internees over the
past few weeks. At 2:00 PM an important meeting was held in
the mess hall to discuss the firewood-cutting order from the
camp commander. There were over forty leading personnel,
including Tanaka-san, in attendance for the meeting. As
nobody wanted to work in the cold for twenty cents a day, they
voted unanimously against supporting the idea.

Tanaka-san presented our objection notice to the camp
commander immediately after the meeting. Upon receiving our
decision, the commander explained that all the other POW
camps in Canada had already enforced mandatory woodcutting. He explained that at present he has no authority to force
any of the internees in Angler to do compulsory work. He said
that he will get an order from the army officials.

November 16, 1943

Four men were released from the camp this afternoon.
Fujimoto-kun was one of them. He was one of my best friends
in the Judo Club and had been one of my best judo partners. I
am going to miss him.

November 25, 1943

The days are getting colder. A fine sleet descends from the grey
skies above. I looked outside and was reminded of a black and
white photograph I once saw, of a military prison set in the fur-

thest reaches of some distant, uninhabitable tundra.

In early 1942 the Canadian government established a contingency regarding the home front during World War II. The Institute of National Selective Service was established. The board of directors was given complete power to delegate the nation's manpower and conscript able-bodied men into compulsory military service.

A rumour is spreading in Angler that the compulsory service might affect the Nisei internees. The tension among us was intensified when we heard that a government agent from Ottawa arrived today to assess the physical condition of the internees for the selective service purpose. We held an emergency meeting in the afternoon to decide on a course of action to protest the sudden government policy.

After some encouraging words from several Issei—Iwamoto-san, Asano-san, and Chiba-san—and a short, angry speech by Nakagawa-san declaring his suggested course of action against the government, we agreed to send a written declaration to the government.

Our notice clearly stated the reasons why we were refusing to co-operate. Since the beginning of the war, the Canadian government had stripped us of our rights as Canadian citizens. The government removed us from our homes and corralled us like cattle, permitting us only those few possessions that we could carry. All of our businesses, houses, farms, automobiles, boats, and furniture had been seized and sold without our consent. We were social outcasts, sent away to deserted mining towns in the interior of BC, and beet farms in Alberta and Manitoba. Our families were shattered when all the Japanese

men between the ages of seventeen and forty-five were ostra-
cized and removed to isolated road camps in the interior of BC
and Ontario. Left behind were beloved wives, children, brothers, sisters, and aged parents. Now the government wants us to
fight for our country? We declared that none of us had any
intention of becoming part of the Canadian Military.

ONE-YEAR YODOKAN
JUDO CLUB ANNIVERSARY

December 5, 1943

I shivered in the freezing wind that descended from the north this morning. I felt very excited today as I walked to the dining hall. The snow that fell two days ago is still frozen solid beneath my feet. It looks like it will remain until next spring. All morning long I was busy helping prepare for the first Angler Yodokan Judo Club anniversary.

Immediately after his release from the Petawawa army detention a year ago, Ishibashi-sensei organized the Angler Yodokan Judo Club. He was helped by the other black-belt holders—Ozaki-san, Kikuta-san, and Kawaguchi-san. We now have a thriving club with over sixty judo participants. A friendly and trustworthy feeling exists between our *sensei* and his students at all times. Every day from 10:00 AM to noon, and 6:00 PM to 8:00 PM, the Yodokan *judoba* in the recreation hall is busy with young men devotedly practicing the art of judo. The scene is enough to inspire the other internees and add some hope to the faltering morale in Angler. I feel very fortunate to have become associated with such a respectable group of men and very privileged to follow the formal instruction of Ishibashi-sensei.

教

へ子ノ部

腰　拂

With the help of the Judo Club members, Matsushita-san and E. Yoshikuni-kun compiled a commemorative book entitled *The Roars of the Great Lakes*. The book holds over 120 sheets bound firmly together between two cardboard covers wrapped in heavy cotton. The handwritten pages contain sketched portraits of some of the judo members, along with some opinions and words of gratitude towards Ishabishi-sensei.

We are all very excited about our one-year Judo Club anniversary. Most of us could hardly wait to see Ishabishi-sensei's face upon receiving his gift. We all felt that our handmade book would be a treasured memento of the Angler Yodokan Judo Club.

At 1:00 PM we gathered in the recreation hall and spoke quietly among ourselves, sipping tea while patiently waiting for Ishabashi-sensei. He arrived shortly thereafter and was welcomed with an elegant speech by K. Yoshikuni-kun. A few members then demonstrated with utmost precision several judo-katas for Ishabashi-sensei. They were enthusiastically applauded as they completed their respectful bows and returned to their seats. Our camp leader, Tanaka-san, addressed our club with a congratulatory speech that praised our productive efforts within the Angler camp. He spoke clearly before the eager crowd:

> Facing the greatest world crisis in history, war in Europe and the Pacific, we countrymen need to make a right decision based on our own cognitive and practical manner. It is important for us to try our very best to keep our morale high, even though we are in a restricted environment. Setting up a judo club in the camp was the most practical way of raising our spirits. Judo not only strengthens the mind and body, but it also teaches us the value of friendship and unity. This earned friendship will last forever. This wonderful memory of friendship will remain deep in your mind until the very day you die.
>
> As you are learning judo, someday you will understand the way of Bushido among the Japanese people. In the Petawawa concentration camp it was just a few men that had begun to practice judo on the sandy ground. It became an incentive for them to begin the judo club in Angler, one year ago. The Angler Yodokan

Judo Club owes its prosperity to the instructors and club members for their excellent efforts in leadership and devotion. Sometime in the future we will be released from this camp and each of us will go in our own direction. Yet the spirit of judo will remain with you to guide you safely along each step of your life. I hope all of you bear this in mind and continue your efforts in practicing judo.

There was thunderous applause, then E. Yoshikuni-kun rose for the anticipated moment. With a heavy silence, all of us sat in our chairs smiling as he presented Ishibashi-sensei with our commemorative book, *The Roars of the Great Lakes*. Ishibashi-sensei remained seated for a moment and then slowly stood up. He seemed overwhelmed. There was a tear in his eye as he thanked us all and said that he felt greatly honoured to have taught such a devoted group of students. He encouraged us to continue with our practice, no matter what happened, and told us that no matter where we were, judo would always be there to help us.

"Progressive and constructive," he said, were two words that he always kept in mind, "Always progress yourself and construct your knowledge, then can you help build a better society and country. Resourcefulness and self-examination are essential in achieving success, while modesty and diligence will give you the strength that you require. Continue your devotion, and you shall deserve your gains." He returned to his seat to the roar of glowing applause.

The ceremony grew more casual in the latter part of the day. E. Yoshikuni-kun continued the celebration with a smooth speech that was followed by an account of the Judo Club's history in the past year. He then introduced the contents of the book *Roars of the Great Lakes*. He even sang a couple of popular Japanese songs in a proud and beautiful voice.

Our party lasted until 4:00 PM. Ishibashi-sensei suggested that our club members meet again in the mess hall after supper. Over 110 men had gathered in the hall to attend the one-year Yodokan Judo Club anniversary. Most of the men in attendance were from our club, but many were Issei supporters and hut-leaders, there to encourage our club.

After supper our club members assembled in the recreation hall. We enjoyed a pleasant evening, relaxed in a friendly atmosphere, talking and laughing together as though we were a big family. Ishibashi-sensei showed us a parcel he had received addressed to our club from the departed Judo Club members Ban-kun and Sato-kun. He opened the parcel and smiled as he read the attached note within. We were all delighted when we saw the many coloured wrappings in the box. We each took a handful of the sweet candies that left a savoury taste in our mouths and a delightful smile on our faces.

December 6, 1943

Abe-san, a good friend of my father's from before the war, was released from Angler today. He was accompanied by three other men, one of whom was O-san. I do not know much about O-san, but from what I can tell, he seems like a gentle man. O-san arrived in Angler as a member of the Mass Evacuation Movement Group but later renounced the group. For reasons unknown to me, he began encouraging the young men in Angler to leave the camp. O-san later became an informer and was seen on several occasions speaking with government officials.

Many of the internees are glad to see him leave.

December 7, 1943

The cloudy weather continues. The snow on the ground has started to melt as the temperatures rise above the freezing mark. The weather is unusually warm for the month of December.

Today is the second anniversary of the start of the Pacific War. I cannot believe that two years have passed since the bombing of Pearl Harbour. I can still vividly remember hearing the shocking Sunday morning radio news as I sat eating at our breakfast table in our rented house in Steveston, BC.

We intended to celebrate the anniversary, but our attempt was curtailed when we received a warning from the camp commander advising us that any demonstrations regarding the war in the Pacific are strictly prohibited.

December 11, 1943

The weather changed for the worse last night when Angler was struck by a violent snowstorm. A guard at the gate told us that the thermometer had plunged to minus thirty degrees.

December 12, 1943

The temperature drops steadily. The piercing wind felt like tiny needles striking my exposed face as I walked across the camp this morning.

Two men advanced to the first-dan black belt today. I myself advanced to the *yon-kyu*, yellow-belt.

December 13, 1943

We received a disturbing announcement from the camp commander. A Selective Service Department official from Ottawa arrived today to impose a government ordinance on the internees in Angler.

He informed the camp commander that he urgently requires six internees to be used as a preliminary trial for the ordinance. He needs the six men to undergo a thorough physical examination and, once completed, to sign a statement declaring that they will co-operate fully with all government orders.

When the six randomly selected men understood what was requested of them, they refused. They were again requested to comply with the camp commander's order, and again they refused. They were all confined to the detention house.

December 23, 1943

I heard the men around me talking about Christmas and New Year cards and was reminded that the end of the year has almost arrived. I looked around and felt that not much had changed in Angler in the past year.

After ten days of confinement, the six men imprisoned for refusing to obey the government order were finally released from the detention house. I doubt that this will be the end of our dispute with the Selective Service ordinance, yet this occasion proved to be a good opportunity to demonstrate to the government our adamant resolve against the discriminate actions towards the Japanese people. We owe a debt of gratitude to these six men for their courageous stand against the camp commander.

We received forty-seven dollars from Kaslo, BC, along with

various presents from Tashme, BC. We also received a New Year's greeting from Kuniyuki Tokugawa, the head of the Japanese Red Cross Society, as well as a greeting card from the International Red Cross Society.

December 24, 1943

As a Christmas event, the movie projector was set up in the recreation hall for us this evening. The call for lights out was postponed until 11:00 PM. The guards seemed happier today, which was nice to see. Japanese people do not care much for Christmas, so for us internees it was business as usual.

I spent the night by myself reading a wonderful biography entitled *My Half Life,* written by Seiji Noma. He gave an amusing account of his wilful and spoiled childhood days in central Japan. Once he had completed his elementary schooling, he decided to go for a higher education in Tokyo. He was in tears when all the villagers came to see him off at the train station. This was his first time away from his village and he felt a momentous emotion, as though he was a young soldier going away to fight a distant war.

It seemed to me a most interesting story and I did not put the book down until I had finished reading. I felt a satisfaction in finding how similar his life was to my own. I began to reminisce about my past. My brother and I had stayed with our aunt and grandparents in a remote village at the foot of the Japanese Appellation Mountains in north-central Japan. Japan had been at war with China for several years already. I had often gone to the train station with a *hi no maru* flag to see our soldiers off to war. In the early spring of 1938, having been brought up by my loving aunt since I was four years old, my turn finally came to leave. My father had travelled from Canada to gather Shig and me to return with him. We would be crossing the vast Pacific Ocean on a great journey to my native land of Canada.

On the day of our departure, the entire community walked with us to the distant train station. I could not hide my excitement as I posed like a proud foreign prince wearing my brand-new suit at the front of the cheering crowd. I had grown up with them for so long, but in that glorious moment I was going on a grand voyage to a strange, faraway land and it was time to say goodbye to all those people that had been so much like a family to me.

I sat on the musty army cot, looking at the book cover in the dimly lit bunkhouse. I was vividly brought back to that day. I looked out of the coach that would take me across the mountains to the big city of Tokyo. Under a clear blue sky, the train whistle blew sharply and the engine began chugging louder. Steam billowed up and a high-pitched squeal emanated from the metal wheels below. We were on our way. I could see all the smiling people, cheering and waving, as they stood on the wooden station platform. I will never forget their genuine happiness for us.

I have no idea when I will ever return to Ichigo, Japan, go back to my carefree childhood village to show those good people my appreciation and that I had become a person that they can be proud of.

December 25, 1943
Today was cloudy and warm.

This is my second Christmas in Angler. Our dining hall was alight with warmth compared to the cold darkness outside. Christmas cheer among the fellow internees and the tinsel decorations in the camp lifted my holiday spirits. We enjoyed a turkey dinner with celery, and a few precious apples and oranges.

As a Christmas gift, we received fourteen decks of playing cards and some Christmas decorations from the YMCA.

December 31, 1943

Angler appears unchanged in its sombre setting on the last day of the year. I did my laundry to get rid of the old year's dirt so that I can at least be wearing some clean clothes when the New Year arrives. I placed a picture of my beloved parents near my pillow and smiled when I realized there was still a good reason to celebrate the New Year.

January 1, 1944

(Kigen 2604, Showa 19.) Happy New Year 1944. The solitary scene of our camp looks like a time-faded painting, completely unchanged by the coming of the New Year.

It was a quiet morning. At 10:00 AM we gathered in the recreation hall to celebrate the New Year. We sang *"Kimi ga yo"* at the opening of the ceremony. Our Japanese national song was followed by an elegant speech by Tanaka-san, encouraging us to keep our unity and wishing us a good year to come. We ended the ceremony at 11:00 AM by singing *"Aikoku koshin kyoku."*

After supper I lay down on my bed and began meditating on the New Year. I am resolved to do many new things this year. Foremost, I want to dedicate myself to achieve greater physical and mental fitness. Secondly, I resolve to correct my retiring personality. I am too shy around others, even to the point of being effeminate. This was my greatest weakness and it must be fixed by the end of the year.

I thought about my aged parents. I am grieved that I can do nothing to help them. I said a prayer for their good health. In the letter I received from my father just before the New Year, he sternly advised my brother and me to remain firm in our beliefs and to not give in to the requests of the government, no matter what they offered. He emphasized that we should continue with our efforts to improve our physical and mental fitness. Three lines in his letter had been censored, but I could guess what he had written. Don't give up. Keep on protesting until the government relinquishes their discriminatory policies against the Japanese people. No matter the cost.

After the evening roll call we gathered in the centre of our hut, each with a bottle of beer in hand, nibbling the cakes and candies we received from the Japanese Canadian communities, enjoying the remainder of the evening at leisure until the call for lights out came at 11:00 PM.

January 2, 1944

It has been a warm day without wind.

At 10:00 AM about eighty judo members gathered in the recreation hall for the first judo practice of the New Year. We had practiced for about an hour when we stopped for a friendly tea party to celebrate the New Year among our club members.

In the afternoon we held our first kendo practice of the year.

January 5, 1944

The cold north wind dropped more snow on our camp overnight. It felt terribly cold outside this morning. It probably felt much colder because of the past few days of warmer weather.

Shig and I received five dollars from Mr. and Mrs. Fujino from Tashme, BC, as a Christmas gift. They were good friends with my father from before the war. For years, every summer Mr. Fujino and his son Tomoe travelled to Skeena River and fished salmon for the months of July and August. The last time I saw them was in 1941, when I went fishing with them off the coast of Vancouver Island. Tomoe-kun caught the largest tiger shark I had ever seen. It must have been over twenty feet long. Fujino-san took his knife and waited for the shark to come up. The large head nuzzled up to the rampart of the boat and Fujino-san firmly raised his knife and sliced into its snout.

January 8, 1944

Some supplies from the exchange ship arrived from Japan today. We enjoyed the taste of *miso* and *shoyu* at our supper table. It was a big treat for us, having gone without our favourite food for so long.

January 9, 1944

At 1:00 PM we held a meeting in the mess hall for the Young Men's Training Group to celebrate the club's one-year anniversary. The attendants were mostly all YMTG members, except for Tanaka-san, Nishimura-san, and Takemura-san who were our honoured guests for their continued support of our YMTG activities. There was a forty-cent admission fee for the informal meeting that paid for the assortment of cookies, cakes, and candies we enjoyed at our tables.

The first part of our meeting was led by Miki-kun as our chairperson. He outlined the progress of our club since its beginning one year ago. Nishimura-san and Takemura-san praised our willingness to learn the intense military drill of Japan. Okubo-kyokan congratulated us for our accomplishments in the past year.

The main attraction was Tanaka-san's amazing account of his thirty-year experience as a Japanese school principal in Canada.

The second part of the meeting was presided over by Kitagawa-kun's more relaxed manner. We were entertained by several excellent singers and musicians. Our meeting ended at 3:00 PM when for a finale we heard a lively tune called the "Angler Marching Song" which had recently been written by Tanaka-san.

January 10, 1944

We received a letter from Suzuki-san and the others who departed for Japan on the last exchange ship. They sent the letter from their ship while crossing the Indian Ocean. The letter mentioned some of the activities onboard the ship and told how they were all very excited and could hardly wait to be back in their homeland, Japan.

A FIREWOOD-CUTTING DISPUTE

January 13, 1944

The camp leader and all hut leaders were requested to attend a meeting with the camp commander today. The commander announced that he had received a compulsory order from army headquarters stating that all internees were obliged to cut and stockpile firewood. The work was scheduled to commence this coming Monday.

After the evening roll call, our hut-leaders informed us about their meeting with the camp commander. Many of us became angry and were soon engaged in a boisterous debate over the order. It did not take us long to decide that we are all solemnly opposed to co-operating with the camp commander's firewood-cutting order.

January 14, 1944

An emergency meeting between the hut leaders was held today. It was unanimously decided that no co-operation will be granted by the internees in regards to the firewood-cutting order.

January 15, 1944

Shortly after our refusal notice was delivered to the camp commander, Tanaka-san, Kimura-san and Wakabayashi-san were asked to meet with the commander in his office. The commander pulled out a letter from behind his desk and folded it to allow only a single paragraph to be read by the three men. When they had finished reading the paragraph, he placed the letter back in his desk and watched them for a moment. The commander told them that this imperative letter had been sent by Colonel Straight, a director of the Internment Operations Department. He admitted that the order was not his idea and that it had been sent directly from the Canadian National Defence. He warned them that it is in their best interest to obey the order or there might be severe consequences.

Our representatives were unmoved. There is some doubt as to the full contents of the letter that they had read. It is suspicious that only a small portion of the letter was shown to them. They requested a written statement from the commander declaring the full nature of the order.

The commander complied by writing them a letter stating that he has received a notice from the National Defence Department in Ottawa that decreed upon all Angler internees a compulsory order to cut firewood for the purpose of camp operations. The work is to commence on January 17, 1944. Ten men from every hut will form a work crew assigned to cut wood from 8:00 AM to 4:30 PM. This order is strictly irrefutable. The letter was signed, "G.C." Most of the internees became grim upon hearing this report.

Later in the day it was discovered that an important portion of our original notice to the camp commander was omitted. We all wondered why and discovered that, having feared certain retribution from the camp commander, Tanaka-san had taken it upon himself to tear out half our notice, effectively removing our statement of declaration against the government's unfair policies towards the Japanese Canadians. The main reason we internees are still in this camp is to protest against the government. We are unwilling to co-operate with the firewood-cutting order imposed by the camp commander until the Canadian government takes a serious look at who we are and why we are locked up like criminals. All of this has been omitted, and only the last half of our notice has been given to the commander, which states only that we want verification of the letter received from the National Defence Department.

Tanaka-san had intended to settle this dispute peacefully. He thought that it would be best to avoid unwanted aggression from the army and at all cost avoid any reoccurrence of the frightening incident that had happened back in Petawawa on July 4, 1942. Then we had been encircled by an army that considered us enemies, and in that dark moment, any wrong movement would have initiated a thundering one-sided firefight. We would have all been mercilessly gunned down. Tanaka-san remembered that he had then alleviated the situation by his quick thinking.

Today his quick thinking had created much animosity towards him. Several internees felt betrayed by his decision to omit the grounds of our declaration. They criticised Tanaka-san for being soft and demanded his immediate resignation.

January 16, 1944

The hut leaders met again today to discuss the firewood-cutting issue. They all agreed to continue supporting our refusal to work.

The hut leaders sent another notice to the commander stating our continued refusal to support the firewood-cutting order. This time, the notice included our grounds for refusal. We are unwilling to engage in any co-operative labour while we remain interned in Angler. We are here to protest against the Canadian government and request that the government end its unfair treatment towards the Japanese community. We are civilians, placed in this camp by the Canadian government. By no means does the army have any right to coerce us into forced labour, as though we are actual prisoners of war. We consider this labour very dangerous. Most internees in the camp have no previous woodcutting experience. To force us to work with an axe in the freezing cold seems most imprudent.

Battle has begun between the internees and the army. I have no idea what kind of punitive actions the army will impose on us. I do not believe they can force any greater punishment on us, as already we have suffered the greatest punishment of being incarcerated behind a barbed wire fence. The only thing I suspect they can do is force us to work at gunpoint. I shudder at the thought. What if even then we refuse to work, would they receive a new compulsory order to shoot us, one by one? Canadians shooting Canadians—I cannot bear the thought.

January 17, 1944

The army has wasted no time. During the night they nailed shut all the doors and windows of our canteen and recreation hall. This was their reply to our notice. They will punish us by taking away our social activities within the camp. Someone remarked that having gone through the evacuation and endless turmoil in the last couple of years, it is funny that they intend to change our minds now by closing our canteen. Shortly after, however, the army reopened the canteen. We talked amongst ourselves about the loss of our indoor activities, judo, kendo, and the YMTG. The recreation hall has been our greatest outlet. I am again reminded of the totality of my internment and how unfair things are.

January 22, 1944
The winds changed to the north in the afternoon, but still the temperatures remain warm for this time of year. There are no more announcements about the firewood-cutting order. We have spoken amongst ourselves and think that this might very well be the silence before the storm.

The closure of the recreation hall is hard on us. We have passed most of our gloomy days in this camp by keeping ourselves busy in the hall with our judo, kendo, and YMTG activities. The days have almost passed by like normal everyday life. Now it is as if the gloom waiting for us in a dark corner had been unleashed upon us in a sudden, vengeful fury, leaving us depleted, in anguish over the emptiness that now consumed our days.

January 24, 1944
A warm south wind has brought unseasonably spring-like weather to Angler, melting some of the snow around us. The misty sky above Lake Superior reminds me again of early spring in Japan.

Our YMT Group assembled outside this morning. We have decided it is best to continue with our training, regardless of the closure of the recreation hall. We exercised by running around the camp perimeter for almost an hour.

We have received over six hundred letters from Japan that arrived with the last exchange ship. But only a handful of the letters belong to the internees living in Angler. The remaining letters are intended for the Japanese communities in BC. I glimpsed at some of the letters that were being opened around me. It is so dear to see some of the postcards from Tokyo bearing the stamps of the Nanko statue. The war has changed Japan in many ways. I noticed that the city Tokyo-shi has become Tokyo-to, a metropolis.

January 25, 1944
It drizzled all night and by morning the compound was transformed into a muddy quagmire. It did not deter us from our running routine. The warm breeze felt good on my face as I splashed through the water puddles on the ground. I felt young and alive, happy to be able to continue my training.

January 26, 1944
The unusually warm weather continues.

The guards have become unfriendly towards us. They walk into our bunkhouses with goggle-eyed expressions and speak bluntly. I suppose they are still feeling resentful about our refusal to cut firewood.

January 27, 1944
The mud puddles turned to ice as the wind changed to the north this morning.

We received a message from the foreign minister of Japan, Mamoru Shigemitsu, expressing a hearty greeting for the New Year. His message said that all the people of Japan wish us good health and continued happiness. We also received seventy dollars from Sandon, BC and a large box of cigarettes from Bay Farm, BC.

January 29, 1944

The hut leaders met this morning and, sadly, our spokesman Tanaka-san handed in his resignation. It came as a surprise to the hut leaders. They had never expected him to resign and asked him to at least wait a while to see just how the internees really feel about him.

Tanaka-san must feel very badly about his mismanagement of the firewood-cutting notice. The criticism he received must have been too much. Granted, he was to blame for having misrepresented us, yet I believe his intentions were purely good. He only did it out of the deepest respect for our well-being, trying at all costs to avoid unnecessary hostility. We really should not resent him for his kind-hearted nature. We should honour him for the strong man that he is, always bearing in mind all the good he had done for us in the past two years, his continued support and constant efforts to keep us together. I believe there is no other man in this camp who could match his leadership ability or equal his fine deportment as our camp spokesman. If he resigns, it will send a shudder through our camp. Hut leaders, and workers in the hospital, kitchen, canteen, post office, and library might even protest his resignation by walking off their jobs. Perhaps he will change his mind.

We sent a telegram replying to the Japanese Foreign Minister's New Year's greeting. We acknowledged his courteous message and expressed our sincere *kansha*. We informed him that we are all in good health and in high spirits and thanked His Excellency for His thoughtful concern. We wished all of the good people of Japan success.

January 30, 1944

We were asked to vote for the acceptance of Tanaka-san's resignation. Only a quarter of the internee population in the camp voted in favour of accepting his resignation. The rest of us formed a majority that rejected his resignation.

Tanaka-san somberly accepted our vote to continue as our camp spokesman. I was very relieved with the result, for I am convinced that he is the best man for the job. He must have been relieved to know that there are still some of us in Angler who wholeheartedly support him.

February 2, 1944

We received ten cents and twelve cigarettes each as a consolation package from Sandon and Bay Farm, Japanese Canadian relocation centres in BC. Shig and I were happy to receive a package of roasted *soramame*, strait beans, and candy from our beloved parents.

February 6, 1944

It snowed intermittently throughout the day, leaving a fine layer of snow upon the frozen ground.

Shig and I received a letter from our close friend Kazuo

Tani-kun in Salmon Arm, BC. I am delighted to see how healthy he looks in the picture he sent us. Only last week I thought about him and wondered if he had changed much since our parting two years ago. I am happy to see from his picture that he has hardly changed at all. He looked the same pleasant, youthful Kazuo that I remember from the time that we worked together in Skeena River.

I am a little surprised and fascinated to see him riding a horse. He looks like a real cowboy, overly proud to be riding on the wild frontier. I grinned and shook my head when I remembered the Kazuo I knew back in Skeena River. We were young and naïve then. We often adventured up the wooded mountains with our rifles, hunting for squirrels and grouse. Other times we strolled by the ocean shore, talking together over the gentle sound of the splashing waves. Now my good friend is far away on a farm, working hard in a place we never knew existed before the war.

He wrote that the farm work is unfamiliar to him but that he has now adjusted well. His employer treats him with a kind respect, which makes him feel very much at ease as he works. His letter seems positive and makes me feel satisfied that my good friend is doing well.

Shig and I looked at his picture for a while and talked about the wonderful times we shared together in Skeena River. I am sad that he is not here with us and wonder when I will ever see him again.

My dear friend,
Thanks for your letter and picture.
I miss you!
The war made us part.
You are outside,
And I am inside
The barbed wire fences.
When will I ever see you again?

Mata aeru hi wa itsu no koto shinyu no,
Shashin natsukashi tessaku no naka.

February 18, 1944
We received a consolation package from the Red Cross Society
in Japan. Inside were many *shakuhachi* bamboo flutes, *Shogi*
chess sets, harmonicas, medicines, and magazines. By the end of
the day the camp had transformed into a jubilant musical con-
cert hall. All around me the sound of sweet Japanese melodies
danced through the air and I imagined I was in a monastery living among the itinerant priests of ancient Japan.

March 19, 1944
Tanaka-san has handed in his resignation again. This time we
are compelled to choose his successor. Kazuo Kobayashi-san
won a majority vote and was appointed as our new spokesman.

March 24, 1944
It snowed all day. Even as the evening approached, the fluffy

snowflakes showed no signs of stopping. The shadows and sounds of the snowflakes touching the windowpanes reminded me of the quiet nights in Ichigo, Japan. Snuggled in my *kotastu* foot warmer, I would listen to my grandmother's gentle stories of old Japan.

A high-ranking official from the Internment Operation Department visited the camp yesterday and asked our spokesman if the internees have changed their stand on the firewood-cutting order. Our spokesman asked him to first reconsider our refusal notice. The official probably expected us to have relinquished our stand against the order once our recreational facility was suspended. Our spokesman informed him that our stand against the order remains unchanged. We are determined to stand behind what we believe and resolve to continue our peaceful war against the government.

April 4, 1944

I read an important article in *The Life Magazine* today entitled "The Japanese American Internment Camps in the US." I realized that we Japanese Canadians, as well as Japanese Americans, are facing a very delicate situation. Having roots in two opposing nations, Japanese Canadians are now compelled to affirm their undivided loyalty to only one nation—Canada or Japan.

Our Japanese parents had emigrated from Japan and we were born as Nisei children in Canada. Would it be necessary for the Nisei children to prove their absolute loyalty to Canada by going to war against their parents' country of Japan?

This regrettable issue brings much anguish to Japanese

Canadians. Some Canadian Niseis were brought up in Japan and still felt a certain loyalty towards their fatherland, Japan. They would rather be deported to Japan. On the other hand, most Niseis had their upbringing in Canada and know very little about Japan. They respect Japan as their ancestors' fatherland but, having been born and raised in Canada, recognize Canada as their true native land. Unless the parents have given their children a formal Japanese education, either at school or at home, it is difficult to convince them to fight for Japan. This kind of pro-Japan family is somewhat rare in Canada. Most Issei parents sent their children to public schools, as they were too busy earning a living. Rarely was Japan a household topic.

All of a sudden the war had started and the Issei parents began preaching to their Nisei children about the Japanese way of life. Canadian-born children had no idea what their parents were talking about and they could not relate. Even if their parents insisted on swearing loyalty to Japan, the children questioned why should they go against their native country of Canada. Many Japanese families suffered dissension and were soon divided.

I believe the future generations of Japanese Canadians will need to carefully consider this important issue.

April 5, 1944

It was cool in the morning. We continued with our morning exercise, running tenaciously over the soggy grass and mud puddles along the barbed wire fencing. Regardless of the weather— thirty below and freezing cold or blowing snow— we still continued to go on our run for about an hour every morning and night. Eventually, Judo Club members, kendo club members, and other internees followed suit. Our running members increased to over eighty strong.

It turned out to be a warm day as the sun rose higher in the sky. We are usually required to stay out of the bunkhouses during the morning inspections. Left on my own, I thought today would be a good day to exercise on the parallel bars. It has been almost six months since I last practiced on the bars. I surprised myself as I looped around the bars with a familiar agility. I continued to swing under the sun, lifting myself higher and faster until with a sharp release I flew upwards and landed firmly on the ground. Some of the men watching me applauded my performance and I bowed playfully, satisfied that my regular exercise has sustained my athletic skill. I carried on with my day with a glow of pride. It feels wonderful that I can finally enjoy the fresh spring air.

SECOND SPRING IN ANGLER

April 7, 1944

At last, spring has arrived in Angler. Beyond the barbed wire fence Lake Superior lies covered under a fine morning mist. The surrounding hills are still covered in snow and beautifully reflect the shining light of our graceful sun. Its golden rays beam down to the foot of the hills, radiating warmth into our fenced compound. The snow is melting away, dripping from the corrugated roofs and forming small streams of water at the base of the whitewashed walls. I can hear the distant cries of seagulls flying far above me, and feel very much embraced by the radiance of spring. My surroundings have been awakened from a long sleep. It is our second spring in Angler.

I practiced on the parallel bars for about an hour, then ran for a while inside the camp perimeter. I enjoyed the touch of the soft ground under my feet. In the afternoon I did some reading and practiced my Japanese handwriting. I did my usual run after the evening roll call, had a cold shower, and then practiced my abdominal respiration before going to bed.

April 11, 1944

Not much snow remains as the warm weather continues.

Some time ago, Kimura-san, the person in charge of the work crews, handed in his resignation. Today we appointed Iwamoto-san as his successor. His responsibilities are to assign internees to the necessary work crews to collect rations from the warehouse, do garbage disposal, kitchen and dining room crews, hospital attendants, unloading coal from the freight cars, and cleaning the army compound.

The person in charge of labour operations for the camp, Iwamoto-san has similar heavy demands as our camp spokesman. There is always an argument with the army as they continuously press us to do extra work for them. We need a firm and diplomatically minded person to handle the demanding position.

April 17, 1944

Our Judo Club members are distressed by the loss of our recreation hall. The hall was the only place available to practice our activities. Most participants are greatly disappointed that they cannot continue practicing their judo. Some of the men have begun practicing on the sandy ground outside.

The ground was dry enough for us to line up outside for our evening roll call. At the sergeant major's command, we advanced six paces forward. The dull sounds of our leather shoes striking the ground brought back memories of this time last year. Seagulls were flying in the twilight sky, far above the shaded hills towards the distant shores. When will this end?

April 19, 1944

Our morning roll call in the fresh air was exceptional.

Koyanagi-kun kicked the ground with his oversized leather shoes and said he was glad that the ground was dry enough to play baseball.

We received a telegram message from the army authority that Shigeru Kuroyama-kun, who had been ailing with appendicitis for a long time, has passed away at the New Denver Hospital.

He was part of our *ganbari ya* group of resistance ever since we were first interned in the Immigration Building two years ago this month. We are all very sad that he has passed away. I pray for his young soul.

April 20, 1944

Mr. Charlie, the government agent, returned to Angler today after his brief absence during the winter months. He was here looking for internees who want to leave Angler, talking about the work available in nearby labour camps. Some internees met with him before he left.

April 24, 1944

Large cumulus clouds rolled in over our camp last night. By morning it had started to rain. The ground is soaking wet and my grey surroundings make me feel homesick. This is the first rainfall of the year.

We were informed today that the recreation hall will be reopened. We let out a great cheer and immediately began making plans to assemble our training groups. A work crew was assigned to clean the hall floors. Many of us hovered by the open doorway looking inside and joking with the men as they cleaned. The familiar air in the recreation hall carried an essence of strength that uplifted my spirits for the entire day.

Major General Alexander from the National Defence Department visited the camp again. His inspection was very brief, as usual.

April 28, 1944

After one hundred days of the recreation-hall closure, the hall was formally reopened today. We are all very excited, knowing that we can finally resume our judo and kendo training.

May 4, 1944

The morning drizzle changed to snow by the afternoon and eventually became a severe snowstorm by the evening. It is surprising to see such a heavy snowfall in May.

I walked over to the library after supper and looked through the wide selection of Japanese and English books. I selected a book entitled *The Shinpuren*. This tragic story tells the story of a samurai family that braved everything to uphold their code during the Tokugawa period of Japan.

May 10, 1944

Lately I have been copying a book entitled *The Ema Style Mind and Body Rebuilding*. Our Judo Club has followed the meditation and breathing exercises described in this book for some time. There are over eighty members and only one book. I was asked to make a copy of the book so that the exercises can be circulated more easily among the members.

I worked at copying this book in my spare time, between

my dining room work duty, YMTG sessions, and judo practice. I am amazed that I was able to perform such a rigourous schedule without becoming fatigued. I believe my exceptional stamina is the result of my regular practice of abdominal respiration. I am happy to note that my devoted practice had helped me become stronger.

May 20, 1944

Koga-kun and I decided to move closer to our friends on the other side of the bunkhouse this afternoon. In all the time of my internment, I have always slept on the top bunk. This time I will bunk on the bottom for a change.

In the close community of internment life, the bunk bed is the only personal place that an internee can call his own. His bunk is his private space, to settle in and find what simple security every man requires. All of his personal belongings are located near his bunk. Pictures of parents, wives, children, brothers, sisters, girlfriends, are all set on a wall or placed on a nearby shelf to serve as a friendly reminder of life outside the camp.

It does not matter to me whether I stayed on the top bunk or move to the bottom bunk. Usually there is more illumination on the top bunk, and I had a better view of everything up top, but the top bunk is also somewhat inconvenient. There are no ladders to climb up and it is more difficult to make my bed in the morning. The elderly people mostly occupy the bottom bunks. People on the bottom bunk have a tendency to get lazy, as it is easier for them to just lie down whenever they want. There are some advantages and disadvantages for both top and bottom bunks. All of these things I considered before the advice of my friend Koyanagi-kun finally helped make up my mind.

I was over on Koyanagi-kun's side of the bunkhouse, talking about bunk beds, when suddenly he said jokingly that if I decide to move over Koga's bed, I was certain to meet with his breaking wind. Koga-kun has a bad habit of releasing wind every time he settles down for bed. From that moment, I took my friend's advice and decided that sleeping on the bottom bunk would provide me with a better atmosphere.

We moved a folding table by the window and made some shelves near our new bunk beds to keep our belongings on. I borrowed part of Koga's shelves as I have so many books and notebooks. I laid down on my bed feeling satisfied with my new arrangement.

May 23, 1944

The days are getting warmer. The faded scenery around the camp is turning into more lively colours. The tamarack trees are budding and flowers are sprouting near the gate.

We played some baseball in the afternoon, but I noticed that we are not as good as we were last year. It is as if we are somehow losing our stamina.

May 27, 1944

The hills and fields surrounding Angler are becoming noticeably greener as the fine warm weather continues.

We began our judo classes for the first time since the recreation hall was closed last January. We discontinued our running exercise this morning and assembled in the recreation hall instead. We practiced judo and kendo for most of the day. It made me a little sad that we have stopped running, but we all feel we have so much catching up to do.

Ever since the recreation hall was closed, Okubo-kyokan, our YMTG leader, has diligently led our running team every day, regardless of weather or circumstance. I am grateful towards

Okubo-san for having trained us despite our isolation and confinement in such a small and dreary place. Many of internees
have him to thank for their improved endurance and physical
well-being.

May 29, 1944
An overcast sky this morning turned to thundershowers by the
afternoon. The heavy downpour of rain is refreshing after the
long dry spell we recently endured.

We received a notice from the camp commander that picture movies will soon be showing again in the recreation hall.

June 3, 1944
More internees have joined our musical exercise sessions that
began a few days ago. We gather on the grounds every morning and evening after roll call and exercise to the music being
played on the camp loudspeakers. Most of the internees are
feeling run-down by the dull internment life. Everyone enjoys
jumping and stretching to the beat of the music, outside in the
open fresh air. This hearty exercise is a welcome change. It is
good to see the elderly people come out and join us. It is much
better for them to be outside in the fresh air rather than lying
in their bunks or playing cards in the stuffy bunkhouses.

June 12, 1944:
The camp commander brought up the firewood-cutting issue
again today. Even though we received a sufficient supply of coal
to survive the last winter, the army was incessant in their pursuit of this unresolved issue. In his address to the internees, the

commander mentioned that in the past he had provided our camp with a wide range of amenities. He had even persuaded the army authorities to reopen the recreation hall so that we were able to enjoy our practices. He now beseeched us to find ten volunteers out of the 400 internees in Angler and form a work crew to go out and cut firewood. He promised that he would continue to provide us with our amenities if we co-operated with the army. He warned that if we refused his request, the army would be compelled to take disciplinary measures and that we would all suffer the consequences. He asked us to carefully considered his offer before giving our reply.

We felt that the camp commander had given us a fair proposal, but still he has threatened us; because of this, we decided to take a vote on the matter.

June 13, 1944

It rained lightly all morning, reminding me of the soft silk rain in Japan.

We voted marginally against co-operating with the camp commander's request. Even though our refusal might trigger another wave of retaliation against us, we still maintain our right to stand against the government.

June 21, 1944

The air is pleasantly refreshed after the heavy rain subsided in the afternoon. The scenery surrounding the camp is vibrant with a lush green colour. I walked over to my favourite spot in the camp and stood silently observing through the fences the delicate flowers that colour the nearby fields.

The picture movie we saw in the afternoon showed a heart-touching scene of fatherly love. An elderly man sitting on a wooden chair next to me wept as he watched it.

June 27, 1944
The dark clouds above Angler look like they are going to pour and thunder at any moment. The air was hot and humid all day.

I injured my right knee while practicing judo the other day. I decided it would be best to hold back from practice for a few days. I asked the chief cook to find a temporary replacement to fill my place as the kitchen fireman until my knee is better. This is the first time in a year that I have requested some time off, since I began working as the kitchen fireman.

June 30, 1944
The men played ball outside all day.

I weighed myself today. I am satisfied to discover that I weigh 130 pounds. I have gained five pounds in the last two months. Having excluded myself from work and practices, I have had more time to read and write.

July 5, 1944
It was drizzling steadily when I awoke this morning. The sky cleared nicely later in the day, permitting the hot summer sun to shine down upon us.

I asked Gune-chan if I could take his place on the work crew for today. It has been almost one full year since I was last outside the camp.

Our work duty was to deliver some ice and window screens

to the army compound. I revelled at the sight of the wild roses, daisies, and countless white, yellow and purple flowers in bloom by the roadside. Their sweet smell stirred my loneliness. I felt very far from home.

On our way back to camp, I stopped for a moment and carefully picked a delicate wildflower up by its roots. When we returned back to our bunkhouse, Maehara-san helped me replant the pink flower in an empty tobacco can. I placed the tranquil flower on my windowsill and someone behind me jokingly exclaimed that he had no idea I was such a dainty guy. I told him that the flower might lighten things up around here.

July 9, 1944

I stopped practicing kendo some time ago as I had too many other things to do. Shig had devoted himself to practicing kendo as his main subject. This afternoon I was invited to watch the first kendo tournament. The recreation hall was filled with excited young men busily practicing their kendo katas. I gave Matsushita-sensei my compliments for his success in accomplishing such tremendous progress in such a short time. Most of the men in the hall were novices less than a year ago. From their agile movements today, they appear quite adept at the art of kendo.

July 20, 1944

Our spokesman, Kobayashi-san, handed in his resignation today. His health is ailing. Tokikazu Tanaka has accepted our request that he be our spokesman again.

July 27, 1944

The rain that has descended upon our camp shows no signs of stopping.

I took some time off from my judo practice today as my arm is still hurting from a recent injury. I copied the Emashiki health system for almost three hours straight this afternoon.

I lay down on my bed after supper and read a book entitled *Aru Otoko*. It is a tender love story. The bunkhouse was quiet this evening. A few men were playing cards at the table in front of me. The sound of the steady rain and quiet music coming from the record player at the far end of the hut, mixed with the love story I was reading, cast a heavy pall of loneliness that made me sink further and further into my bunk.

I suddenly sprang to my feet and took out my mandolin, determined to throw off my melancholy. I stamped my foot lightly and my fingers began strumming a sweet classical melody. The card players stopped to look up. One of them reached for his harmonica and began playing high and low notes that sounded like a choo-choo train. The card players began tapping the table with their hands, drumming a gentle rhythm. One of them whistled in harmony. As the rain continued to pour down outside, our music filled the bunkhouse, faster and faster, louder and louder until some of the men were up on their feet, clapping and dancing together. Just as suddenly as the music had begun, it all too suddenly stopped and we resumed our monotonous existence. The card players sat down and played their cards. I picked up my book and began reading where I had left off, smiling, still hearing the sweet melody in my head.

July 29, 1944

The grey weather continues. It is only the middle of summer and once again it feels like fall.

Our YMTG exercises will soon be completed. Our instructor Okubo-san says that we are all good enough at our military drill. I am also almost finished copying the Emashiki technique book for the Judo Club. What should I study next in my free time? There is so much that I need to study—English, mathematics, and music. My Japanese handwriting is not good enough. I should concentrate more time in developing my proficiency.

I allow much of my time to be wasted, in vain, with little regard for the integrity of my existence. Some people may say that if you think of life as being serious, like the philosopher, you may end up a very solitary and cynical man. They might suggest one should accept life as it comes and not to worry. I think that if people take their life easy and live carefree, there will be no improvements to our human race because everyone will be too busy living the easy life. Our race has produced many great religious figures in history. Christ, Buddha, and Mohammed are all important men, because they considered their lives seriously and looked deeply within themselves to find the wisdom of their souls.

I believe that this insight deserves more attention, and that I would greatly benefit by studying more about this serious matter of existence.

August 6, 1944

An unfortunate accident occurred this morning while huts 3-A and 2-B were playing a softball tournament. The baseball bat slipped out of a player's hand and struck Kazuo Nishimura-kun right on the forehead. He had been keeping score on the nearby embankment. He regained consciousness shortly after he was brought to the infirmary. We took the precaution of sending him to the Port Arthur Hospital, as we feared that he might have suffered a skull fracture.

August 7, 1944

Today we obtained permission to go outside Angler in search of some makeshift wooden posts. Our intention is to construct more parallel bars for internees to exercise on. The four of us left our hut with Okubo-san as our leader and set out towards the eastern hillside. We were accompanied by a guard, of course.

It was a beautiful, sunny afternoon. The hills and surrounding fields were covered in a verdant growth that released a rejuvenating air of freshness. I remarked how completely different the outside atmosphere was from that within the barbed wire enclosure. We were taking our time, talking casually among ourselves while enjoying the peacefulness of our surroundings. We walked for about an hour before Gune pointed to a cluster of trees that would be suitable for our needs. We cut them down and dragged them to the roadside.

Our appointed time of return was not until 4:00 PM so we took our time returning. I stumbled upon a small patch of blueberries and I called to Gune. Soon all of us were busy picking and eating the sweet berries, eagerly crowding around the small bush like a pack of famished children. We searched the bushes,

pretending to look for more trees to cut down, all the while eating lots of berries and enjoying a delightful moment of freedom.

We wanted to stay outside for as long as we could, and
were sorely disappointed when the guard called for us to return
to camp. He shook his head when we asked to stay outside
longer and stated that an official from the Internment
Operation Department was scheduled to give us an inspection
this afternoon.

August 8, 1944

It showered in the morning. By noon the sky had cleared nicely,
allowing for a warm sun to come out. I joined a work crew
again today. We raked the perimeter of the camp and pulled
weeds from between the barbed wire fences. We actually spent
more time picking blueberries than pulling weeds.

I returned to the bunkhouse when we had completed our
work duty and returned to copying the Emashiki technique. Just
as I opened my notebook, someone informed me that a parcel
was waiting for me at the canteen. It is such a great joy to receive
a parcel in this mirthless camp. Shig and I hastily opened our
parcel and discovered some good *sora mame*, roasted straight
beans. We lifted them out and found a letter from my father,
mixed in with some packages of chewing gum, chocolates, some
cookies and *endo mame*, roasted green peas.

August 9, 1944

It rained off and on all day long. I read a book entitled *Shisen
o Koite, Over the Dead Line*. It was a powerful true story about
a man who fought for his survival, never giving up until the

very end. I was reminded of many things by this book. Even if a man finds himself in a hopeless situation, he can always find a way out, as long as his will is completely determined. The moment he loses hope, he loses his will to fight and he will surely perish. Regardless of his situation, as long as he has hope in his heart, he will always have a chance to get out from whatever perilous situation besets him.

August 13, 1944

At 1:00 PM we held an *Obon Hoyo,* a Buddhist service, for the Feast of Lanterns in the recreation hall. We prayed for the families of the soldiers who have died in both world wars. We also prayed for the four dead German POWs buried on the eastern hillside.

Reverend Matsubayashi began chanting a Buddhist Sutra-Chant. Tanaka-san stood before us and spoke a few ceremonial words. Reverend Matsubayashi then began his sermon. He preached that Buddha could only be received by achieving the state of Nirvana. Most of his sermon was incomprehensible, however, as he used many archaic Buddhist words. Homegrown vegetables, wildflowers, cakes, and soft drinks had been set before a statue of Budda at the front of the hall. The service ended near 3:00 PM.

This evening I began reading a book entitled *Inja No Unmei, A Destiny of a Hermit,* written by Mushakoji. I found it somewhat dull at the beginning, but as I continued to read I became completely engrossed in the story. Before long it was well past 11:00 PM and a guard was excitedly shining his flashlight through my window, motioning for lights out.

There was an interesting conversation in the book between a hermit and a hedonist. The hedonist asked, why does our human race need to work so hard, why does our human race have to suffer, and why does our human race have to avoid pleasure? The hermit replied that we were born to this Earth to acknowledge the true meaning of our existence. Our only true reward was our continued survival. For that reason, man is compelled to work hard, and avoid those pleasures that work against his existence.

I was impressed with the words of the hermit. For many years, mankind has worked hard to survive the perils of nature. He has tamed the animals around him and constructed monumental shelters to keep him from danger. Also, man has loved his pleasures, which usually seem to work against him. If man is to survive, man should make every effort to work towards his continued survival.

BLUEBERRY PICKING

August 17, 1944

The days are getting shorter. Dark clouds loomed over Angler in the morning. By noon a northern wind blew across the fields, dispersing the clouds and sending them gently adrift towards the distant horizon.

Today was a perfect day to be outside on a work crew. At around 9:00 AM five of us who are close friends—Okazaki-kun, Koga-kun, Oyama-kun, Kawahira-kun, and myself—accompanied by a guard, left the camp gate and headed for the army compound to obtain our work assignment from the quartermaster, Captain Kaye. We were all very pleased when he assigned our crew to dig a garbage pit on the outskirts of the camp. This is the easiest work duty; we knew well we could work at our leisure. Gune-chan whistled merrily as we walked over to the tool shed to collect our shovels.

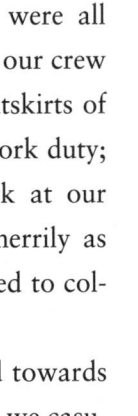

We headed down the road towards the job site, taking our time as we casually picked ripened blueberries along the way. When we arrived, the kind French Canadian guard gave us the depth and width measurements of the pit we were to dig. Okazaki-kun and Kawakira-kun volunteered to stay behind and dig the pit while Koga-kun, Oyama-kun and I hurriedly left them to go gather more blueberries.

Everywhere I looked, the bushes were full of ripened berries ready to be picked and eaten. This remote part of the country is sparsely populated and the only ones around to feast on the berries are the birds and bears. Year after year, autumn after autumn, an endless amount of berries ripen and fall to the ground, until the next season comes and the small bushes produced berries again. The guard mentioned that the berries would be worth as much as thirty cents a pound at the market.

Beautiful colours surrounded us. Autumn is the best time of year for all the birds and animals. There is an abundance of food for them to gather before the long, cruel winter blankets the land. Even in this desolate region, Mother Nature provides a paradise for all living things. All living things are equally blessed by her generous hands. It would be a wonderful world if man could learn from nature.

We used our caps to gather berries and when we had filled them, we used Koga-kun's sweater to gather even more berries. The bushes were still wet from the morning dew. Pesky mosquitoes came out at us like fighter planes buzzing madly at unexpected intruders. It was too much for Koga-kun. He dashed back to the pit and took over Kawahira-kun's shovel. Gune-chan was happy to join us. I found it strange how the mosquitoes left him alone. We joked about what kind of soap he was using. But none of us felt overly bothered as we continued picking and eating the berries.

We were preoccupied by our enjoyable pursuit, and moved further and further into the forest. The good-natured guard remained at our side, not seeming to mind too much. Lost in the tangle of bushes, momentarily distracted by the untamed forest, I forgot about the world around me. Within this hidden grove, there was no war, no barbed wire fence, nor did I mind the red-patched POW uniform that clung to my shoulders. Alive within a hearty wilderness and laughing with my companions, I felt completed within nature's heavenly womb, completely blessed by the warmth of her giving hands.

When we returned to camp we had more than twenty pounds of blueberries. News of our berrypicking adventure quickly spread in the camp and suddenly everyone wanted to go outside and pick berries. We negotiated with the army personnel, asking them to allow a few internees to go out and pick berries every day. In return for their permission, we will give them half of our take.

August 28, 1944

The end of summer feels very close. The evenings are getting considerably cooler. Nishimura-kun, the ball player injured during the other's day tournament, returned to camp from the Port Arthur Hospital. There is a small dent on his forehead where he was hit with the bat, but otherwise he seems fine.

I finally completed copying the book *Emashiki Health Method*. It runs to more than 240 pages and took me a full three months to complete.

September 29, 1944

The scenery surrounding our camp has turned to autumn colours. After last week's heavy frost, most of the wildflowers near the fences have disappeared, leaving behind only the wild daisies to stand resolutely, lonesomely defiant.

Yesterday I was assigned to the evening Judo Club to assist Ozaki-san with the training. I was happy to be in the evening class. It gave me something to do and freed up time during the day for my academic studies.

Ozaki-san is an excellent judo-ka, nidan black belt, bright and energetic. He is forty and a small man, no more than five feet one inch in height, and weighing no more than 120 pounds. His physique is extraordinary. His highly trained body moves with lightning agility. He can throw an opponent weighing twice his weight over his head with complete ease.

His favourite *waza* are in the lying position. He can use his centre of gravity far better on the mat. It is not easy to hold him down. He moves like a cat, turning and twisting with a flowing grace. Eventually, his momentum will place him on top of his opponent. With a sudden ferocity he pins him down with an arm lock or chokehold. Whenever he pinned me down on the mat, it felt like he weighed 200 pounds instead of a mere 120 pounds.

I learned valuable lessons from him. He taught me never to work against an opponent's strength. Instead, I should use my opponent's momentum as a means to pull him off balance and then throw him or lock him down.

December 20, 1944

We held a year-end judo grade-advancement tournament the

other day. I did very well. I ended the day with two wins, two ties and one loss. My *newaza*, lying down position, was exceptionally good. I pinned both of my opponents down on the mat. I even received praise from Ishibashi-sensei. I owe my proficiency in judo to Ozaki-san's thorough instruction.

Before we began our judo practice this morning, Ishibashi-sensei announced the grade advancements. Three members advanced to black belt. I am happy to receive my brown belt. I had advanced to the *ikkyu* level and am now a black-belt candidate.

January 1, 1945

We spent a very quiet Christmas and New Year. This is our third New Year in Angler. Even in this monotonous internment life, surprisingly enough, the time seems to pass by quickly.

Not many changes have occurred in the past year, except for the population in the camp: it has decreased to 430 *ganbari-ya*. Once we were over 700 strong.

The only real change I notice around me is my neighbour Maehara-san. When I got up this morning I saw he had shaved his old Chinese-style moustache and beard, which he has had since the beginning of his internment over three years ago. I said to him, with some surprise, that he looked much younger. With a grin he winked at me and replied that the change was good and he expected a big change in Angler this year.

January 2, 1945

The Japanese believe that a fresh start in the beginning of the year is very important. The first day of practice for Japanese sports—judo, kendo, and sumo—usually started on the second day of January. Every year, our Angler judo and kendo clubs have followed this tradition.

After breakfast a few of the club members carried some water and brooms to clean the *dojo-ba* in the recreation hall. I was given the job of supervising the mending and patching of the *dojo-ba's* canvas mat. Our mats were getting old, worn out after so many heavy practices day after day, morning through evening. We do not receive any replacements. The YMCA supplied us with some canvas material to cover the mats and protect them from further tearing.

At 10:00 AM all the Judo Club members gathered in the *dojo-ba* for their first day of judo practice. The hall was much warmer than the sub-zero temperature outside. I was astonished to see all their bright and enthusiastic faces, their bodies all clad in freshly washed bright white *judo-gis*.

Their *judo-gis* were showing some wear and tear from the many months of heavy use. Most of the wear occurs around the collars and sleeves. We use twine to stitch over the torn material. The material from flour and oatmeal bags taken from the kitchen made good *judo-gi* pants.

February 17, 1945

The cold season that has locked us in ice these past four months has finally begun to loosen its icy winter grip. A powdery snow falls gently from the ashen sky.

I joined a Haiku club today. It is organized by Bunjiro Tanaka-san, and has fifteen participants. We are to meet once a week in the mess hall to compose seventeen-syllable Japanese poems together. The theme for today's haiku was the wintry sky.

A wintry sky presses above the Rooftops,
The snow fast Approaching.
A train whistle echoes Heavily,
Into the wintry sky.

Fuyuzora ya yane o asshite yuki chikashi,
Fuyuzora ye kisha no kiteki omota geni.

May 15, 1945

Another spring has arrived in Angler. It is my third spring here. The remaining snow on the mountaintops has almost completely melted away. Looking beyond the barbed wire fence, I can see the tamarack trees starting to bud again. A warm southern wind carries the pleasant whistle of a train passing nearby.

I am finally able to breathe in the open air again. As the days grow warmer, my muscles are more relaxed and I start to forget about the long winter of stuffy isolation. The months seem to be going by quickly, even though I am locked inside this dreary concentration camp. It is hard to believe that I have already passed three winters here. This camp can be treacherous if there is nothing to do. Time seems to have stopped. I am fortunate that I have so many interests and my time is put to some good use. I cannot help but feel sorry for those men around me who drag themselves through their days. I congratulate myself for having found so many things to keep me busy during my confinement, so much so that I barely have enough time to wash up before bed.

The ancient saying is so true: time is like a great flowing river, never stopping to wait. Even a second of time is more precious than gold and should be embraced with all honour and purpose.

June 2, 1945

The trees around the camp are greener as spring is again in bloom. Several internees began constructing mandolins this past month. The most important part in a mandolin is the bottom drum section. The thickness of the material used for the drum construction and the position of the small divider inside the drum decides the quality of sound the instrument will make.

July 15, 1945

The fine weather continues. I took a break from my studies today to suntan for a while in the afternoon with Koyanagi-kun, my judo partner. I lay calmly on the sand, looking up at the open sky. My thoughts went back to my childhood memories in Ichigo, Japan. I found myself dressed in my kimono, walking barefoot beside a mountainside ricefield. In the sun-filled valley, I could hear the sound of trickling spring water coming down from the mountains, falling gently to nourish my village's ricepads.

A couple of haiku verses have come to mind. On our next meeting, I will propose that our haiku theme be spring water.

A trickling spring water from the
Meadow,
Sparkling in the summer sun.
Cool spring waterspouts out from
Under the shaded trees,
Where sunrays seep through.

Choro-Choro to kusa moru
Shimizu hi ni hikaru.
Hamore-bi no shizukeki kokage
Ya waku shimizu.

July 17, 1945

I was scheduled to join the work crew again today. It was a good day for unloading the coal from the freight cars. The sun was hidden from our backs by a cloudy, windswept sky. Four of us worked quickly and finished unloading the coal early. I picked some wild roses from the roadside as we walked back to camp and later placed them on a shelf near my bed.

July 21, 1945

The other day we received an order from the regiment adjutant stating that a night watchman was to be appointed for each bunkhouse. We do not understand why they want a night watchman in the middle of summer, as our stoves are not lit and there is no fire hazard.

I am required to fill the position for tonight. I have to stay awake and watch our hut from 10:00 PM to 6:00 AM. A guard entered our hut on his routine patrol every hour from 10:00 PM until 1:00 AM. After that he went to bed, and I did not see him anymore. I have been left alone. All I can hear are the sounds of the sleeping men around me. There is no one to talk to. I just sit quietly on my chair by the boiler in the corner of the wash-room and try my best to stay awake. During the early part of the night, I wrote down some judo techniques and worked on my next haiku.

The morning hours elapsed. The silence grew heavier and my awareness slowly began to recede. I wrestled with sleep, my eyes opening and closing and my head bobbing up and down. I dreamed that I was on an island, basking in the tropical sun on a warm sandy beach and leaning against a tall palm tree. The ocean wind gently caressed my hair and the sound of flowing waves gave me an air of weightless calm. Three fighter planes emerged suddenly from the treeline behind me, flying fast and casting a howling shadow on the sandy shore.

I was startled awake. I quickly glanced around the sleeping room, and wondered how long I had been asleep. I got up and walked around the bunkhouse for a while and was glad to see the light of dawn touch upon our windows. I knew then that morning had finally come.

THE END OF THE WAR

August 10, 1945

"Japan has surrendered! Japan has surrendered!" a guard shouted at the gate. All of us ran out onto the grounds and crowded around the gate. A guard told us that the war in the Pacific is over; the Japanese Empire surrendered yesterday. The news shocked us all. Most of us still believed that the Japanese Empire would win the war. I shook my head in disbelief.

August 17, 1945

The headlines in the newspaper announced that the Japanese government has signed a surrender agreement with the United States. The paper mentioned that the dropping of atom bombs quickened the war's end. A picture of Emperor Hirohito was taken as he addressed the Japanese people on the outlines of the armistice. All around, the internees dropped their heads as they read the news. I knew that they had believed Japan was winning the war and I guessed that they were thinking how this would affect their plans to return to Japan.

August 20, 1945

We were able to hear more up-to-date news. A radio receiver

was brought into the camp today. The news announced that a team of sixteen Japanese delegates have arrived in Manila to discuss the armistice treaty with General McArthur.

September 5, 1945
The warm, humid days continue.

The headlines in the newspaper announce that the Japanese delegates have signed an armistice agreement at Tokyo Harbour. All day long the radio buzzed with the news of Japan's ultimate surrender.

September 12, 1945
The weather pattern suddenly changed over night. I was surprised to see a cover of frost on the ground this morning. The cold wind announces the arrival of winter.

A rumour is spreading that every internee in Angler will soon be repatriated to Japan. If the rumour is correct, all of us may be spending the coming winter in Japan.

October 17, 1945
The autumn season deepens and the leaves on the trees around the camp are almost gone. Winter is on our doorsteps. I began a Japanese shorthand lesson today.

November 17, 1945
The snow that fell a couple days ago remains frozen on the ground. The cold weather continues. I decided not to attend the judo tournament this morning as I felt sick and fevered. I did however attend our haiku meeting in the afternoon. The

haiku theme for today was the remaining snow.

I harvest some marsh parsley by
the small creek
Where still some snow remains.
The fresh raking marks on the
Remaining
Snow.
After someone has swept
Away the pine needles.

*Yuki nokoru ogawa no hotori ya seri o
toru.*
*Zansetsu ni kumade no ato ya matsu-
ba-kaki.*

November 27, 1945
The winter cold keeps us indoors. According to a newspaper report, the repatriation of Japanese Canadians is scheduled to commence in January of 1946. As of yet we had heard nothing of the Canadian government's intentions regarding the internees in Angler. It seems almost certain that we will be repatriated to Japan, sooner or later.

December 1, 1945
A newspaper announced that the first group of Japanese

Canadians will begin repatriation on January 17, 1946. They will each receive two hundred dollars for personal spending money on their voyage back to Japan.

December 9, 1945

The temperature dropped steadily last night. The wind blew snow around the camp all day. There was an article in the newspaper about Japanese Canadian Nisei. According to the paper, the decision to be repatriated to Japan will be left entirely up to individual Canadian Nisei.

I agreed with Ishibashi-sensei when he said it would be best to remain in Canada until Japan becomes more stabilized. He believes it is not a good idea to return to Japan now as the country is facing extreme hardships and confusion from all that it has recently suffered.

A few judo members have vowed to return to Japan, regardless. Most of us agree that it is best to remain in Canada for the time being.

As for my brother and me, our future depends entirely on the actions of our parents. If they decide to return to Japan, we will honour their decision and return with them. I spoke with Shig about our situation then sat down and wrote my parents a letter to ask them their intentions.

December 11, 1945

Winter has locked us in ice once more. It was minus thirty degrees this morning. The canvas-covered mats we use for our judo practice are frozen hard. The two stoves in the hall do little to provide us with any warmth. Even though I was coated in sweat after a few rounds of judo practices, the tips of my toes grew numb from the penetrating cold.

Before the end of the war, the internees were all set on constructing their mandolins. Now their tools are turned to making suitcases. All day long I could hear the sounds of hammers and saws working steadily in the bunkhouses.

December 18, 1945

It was a clear, crisp day. The freezing cold continues. Less sunlight penetrated into our bunkhouse as more ice built up on the windowpanes.

We received an order from the army authority today. They request that our spokesman Tanaka-san resign his position immediately. We refuse to obey their order. We feel that Tanaka-san is our elected spokesman. He was elected by us internees to speak on our behalf. We are appalled that the army would make such an iniquitous request. Our assistant spokesman Suzuta-san was sent to determine why they had made such an order. He was unable to get an answer from the regimental adjutant and was told only that an answer will be given as soon as a new spokesman is appointed.

Since news arrived of the Japanese surrender, the army has adopted an air of arrogance towards us. They sneer haughtily and speak to us as though we are boys who know no better. Tanaka-san must not have appreciated this. They probably want someone more servile to deal with.

December 25, 1945

We were allowed to sleep in until 8:30 this morning. It has been a worrisome and uneasy Christmas in Angler. Wavering feelings of indecision haunt the internees, reminding me of how it was back in December 1941 when the threat of a Pacific War was talked about throughout the Japanese community.

Our individual futures, for the first time in many years, were very grim. For the last four years we have been given very few choices to make for ourselves. Now, with Japan defeated, the camp will be closing down. With no word on the government policy towards the internees, we have been handed the heavy burden of choosing between remaining in Canada or being repatriated to Japan.

We were served a customary turkey dinner for our late, 10:00 AM breakfast. Apples and cakes, purchased from our canteen funds, were set at our tables. A couple of motion pictures were shown in the recreation hall between 11:00 AM and 3:00 PM. I left early as I had already seen them before. We skipped our lunch and quietly enjoyed an early Japanese-style supper with rice, miso soup and miso-based pork. There was no evening roll call and the lights out time was postponed until 10:30 PM.

December 30, 1945

A strong wind blew a cloud of snow high above Angler.

As the end of 1945 approached, I did all my laundry and tidied up my place in the bunkhouse to prepare for the New Year.

Our judo members met in the recreation hall to pass the time that remained and make the parting year go by faster. We brought along our own soft drinks, apples and candies, and spent a friendly afternoon talking and laughing together. This might be our last club meeting together in Angler, as we expect that the call for the camp closure might come any day now.

December 31, 1945

On a windy day, the ancients in Japan would say it was a *shihazu kaze*, the cold year-end wind. In Angler, the cold year-end wind feels as though it penetrates right through a man. It was a freezing experience this morning when I was required to carry pails of water from the bunkhouse to help clean the recreation hall.

Another year has passed and the scenery in Angler looks the same. A friend of mine smiled at me as he slowly scratched an X on his homemade calendar. There was little else to indicate that an entire year had gone by and another year was about to begin.

We assembled in the recreation hall after the evening roll call and watched a colour movie entitled *Home in Indiana*. I was sad as I watched the heartwarming scenes, feeling as though I had somehow gotten lost and would never find my way back home. We played bingo games until midnight and then were sent back to our bunkhouses for lights out.

January 1, 1946

The air was very still and cold this morning.

We celebrated our fourth New Year in Angler. We ate delicious *manju*, bean jam on a bun, that was made by our kitchen staff. It was some comfort to know that this will probably be the last New Year that we are imprisoned within this concentration camp. It is impossible to predict what will become of us this

coming year. I watched the listless men around me and knew that none of them has decided whether to remain in Canada or leave to Japan.

I thought back on all the days I have lived within this camp and congratulated myself for having upheld my personal honour. When I first arrived in Angler, three and a half years ago, I was very young. Looking back, I was timid and uncertain about my own strengths. As the days passed by, I grew determined to make the best of my time. Every day I looked for something new to learn.

My unyielding devotion to my studies and training have rewarded me and today I am a richer man than I was before the war. I feel good knowing that I am strong and that I am fully prepared for whatever future lies before me.

March 7, 1946

It rained last night, the first rainfall of the year. The rain and melting snow have left puddles on the ground. The sky cleared up in the afternoon and the world around us basked in a warm spring sun.

For us Japanese Canadians, however, dark clouds continue to hover ominously over us, as our future is undetermined. We are in a dilemma as to what direction we should take. If we remain in Canada, we will endure still more judgements by Canadians and have to begin our lives all over again. If we leave Canada, we will be faced with the sadness and fear of a broken Japan.

A government agent from Ottawa will arrive soon to inquire about our decisions. All those internees who want to remain in Canada will be released almost immediately from Angler. Those wishing to leave Canada will remain in Angler until arrangements are made for their transport to Japan.

March 12, 1946

A government agent posted some job openings for those internees wishing to remain in Canada. The jobs are mostly in eastern Canada. There are some jobs available on sugar-beet farms in Alberta and Manitoba.

After lunch we held a farewell party for Ishibashi-sensei and the other Judo Club members: Marubashi-san, Ozaki-san, Oseko-san, Morita-san, and Yoshida-san. They will depart for work camps in eastern Canada within a few days.

Ishibashi-sensei was teary eyed as he made his farewell address to us. It was sad to hear him say goodbye. Yoshikuni-kun shook his hand and spoke a few words of praise, but his speech soon faltered. Even though the atmosphere of our parting was very sad, we managed to spend the remainder of our time together in a friendly manner. We sipped our soft drinks and ate candies, encouraging each other to be strong for the future. Before parting, we sang *"Otoko no inochi"* together.

The camp is now divided into three groups—the repatriating group, the remaining group, and the undecided group. There is no ill feeling between our groups. Opinions no longer have a place in Angler. It is a difficult time for each of us as we are faced with a hard personal choice.

March 14, 1946

It is a nice warm day, a welcome change from the cool weather of late. Thirty-nine men were released from the camp today.

At 2:00 PM I went to the gate to see my friends off.

March 15, 1946

Most of the fifteen men leaving today are going to Toronto or the Hamilton area. Ishibashi-sensei is among them. I was assigned on a work crew, responsible for unloading food rations from the freight cars at the train station.

I was happy to meet with Ishibashi-san outside the train station. I walked up to him and shook his hand as he embraced my shoulder. We have lived together for almost four years. He has been like a father to me, at times like a brother. He has shown me my own strength and taught me how to stay sharp and calm, to wait for the right moment with patience. I feel only sorrow in this moment. I feel as if my older brother is going far away, and I will not see him perhaps for a long time. I once read that meetings and partings are a natural occurrence in our lives. Parting from a close friend is to me the worst experience in my life.

He boarded the train this afternoon. Our eyes met and for a brief moment we shared a solid understanding, and then he was gone. I ran beside the moving train, shouting through my tears, "Please stay in good health!" I saw his hand wave to me from the coach window. I remained standing on the wooden platform long after the train had disappeared behind the hills. I vowed to myself to always remember what my good friend had done for me during our long years of internment together.

Our Judo Club seemed very empty without Ishibashi-sensei. Eiichi Yoshikuni-kun tried to encourage us, but it was not the same.

A LETTER OF DECISION

March 22, 1946

A new spring has arrived to our solitary camp. The trees are not yet in bloom, but the warm sunlight descending from the emerald sky and the birds chirping merrily in the spring air is enough to cast away the shadows of uncertainty that cloud my heart.

Shig and I have made up our minds to remain in Canada. We received a letter from our parents stating their decision to stay in Canada until Japan is more stable. My mind is finally at ease. We will honour our parents by remaining with them in Canada. Without any further delay, we made our application to leave Angler.

Even though I have finally made my decision to remain in Canada, my future is still very uncertain. It is as if I am floating on a ship through impenetrable fog, and must wait until I finally land ashore.

I thought about what I can do, and what I can expect. I knew that the Japanese Canadian Issei have worked hard to establish themselves within Canada. Their hard-won foundations are now completely lost. We will have to work hard again to regain all that the Issei and Nisei have long worked for. It is crucial for the Nisei who remain in Canada to find the strength to rebuild a lasting foundation for the Sansei and Yonsei of our future generations.

April 1, 1946

A severe thunderstorm passed over Angler this afternoon, pelting the camp with hail. An RCMP officer arrived to interview the internees who are to remain in Canada. There are sixty-five names on his list.

I had an interesting conversation with O-kun today. I always enjoy talking with O-kun and respect his deliberative manner. We spoke at length about the benefits and detriments of remaining in Canada, or repatriating to Japan. He shared his sentiments regarding Japan. He argued that Japan now needs our young strength to rebuild its collapsed empire. I stated to him that Canada is the country that our parents chose, and that we should remain here and rebuild a foundation for our families. So absorbed had we become in our conversation that it was not until 2:00 AM that we paused for a moment. He turned to his bedside shelf and handed me a letter to read.

It was a letter from his father, living in a relocation centre in British Columbia. The letter had many kind words for his O-Kun, and was written on a happy note as father and son will soon be reunited. I looked up at O-kun for a moment before continuing to read his letter:

Japan fought her war for her own reasons, and lost. All of her empire is destroyed, yet given the strength of her people, in time she will rebuild herself. Many years ago, you were brought to this country so you and your family could have a future that was unhindered by aggression and despair. This country was my gift to you. Dear son, I ask that you come home to stay with me.

I was deeply touched by the words. I folded the letter and returned it to O-kun.

We were silent together for a long time, just looking at each other in the dim light of our bunkhouse and thinking. Finally, he said to me that he accepted the words of his father. He told me that the letter spoke the truth and that he would remain in Canada to care for his family. I placed my hand on his shoulder and looked firmly into his eyes. We had shared many words together in this bunkhouse, but never before this day had I felt like a true *ganbari ya*.

April 3, 1946

It is a cold day. Small, drifting snowflakes descend silently from the ashen sky. I was shaking as I walked in the frigid wind towards the gate to say goodbye to my departing friends. It was heartbreaking to see Koyanagi-kun standing in the group of men huddled around a collection of baggage.

Since the time we were confined together in the Immigration Building, almost four years ago, we had shared many days together. Some of the moments we had were good, and other moments were not so good. I stood there with them by the gate and was at a loss for words as I looked at their tear-stained faces. It felt like I was being separated from my family all over again.

Finally the time came for them to leave. One by one they were escorted through the gate. They turned a few times to look back at the camp that had sheltered them for so long. I raised my hand as they receded into the distance and whispered "*Ganbari ya,* dear friends; never give up."

My head was low when I returned to the bunkhouse and I saw the empty beds that had once belonged to my good friends. I could not help but feel sad when I thought that each day, one by one, I was losing my brothers.

April 9, 1946

The snow that fell yesterday lies frozen on the ground. The wind makes it feel like it is mid-winter.

Eight men were released from the camp today. They were mostly elderly Isseis. I received a letter from Ryoichi Nakashima. He stated in his letter that it had taken a while for him to adjust to the hard working conditions of the Port Arthur bush camp, but finally he has begun to enjoy his freedom. He plans to move to Fort William or Toronto once his six-month contract is over.

April 16, 1946

I read a book entitled *The Great Flood* today. This book describes the interesting story of a brilliant young Polish knight

who fought for the independence of his home country during the war-torn years of the seventeenth century.

I found the European setting fascinating and was pleased to note that the people strongly believed in a code of honour.

April 24, 1946

Shig and I, along with a few other men, were called to meet with the government agent in his office near the gate. Charlie is a familiar face in Angler. He gave us a description of a job opening in a pulpwood bush camp near Winnipeg, Manitoba. We asked him for some time to consider his offer.

April 25, 1946

The Nishimura brothers, Kitamura-kun, my brother, and I discussed the job being offered us and, after some deliberation, decided that we will accept the six-month contract. In the afternoon the five of us walked over to see the agent and signed the agreement.

April 26, 1946

Shig and I began packing our homemade suitcases. Our departure date is set for April 29. I am surprised to see how much stuff we have accumulated in the time we have been interned in Angler. We have three suitcases between us, full of miscellaneous belongings—letters, pictures, books, woodcrafts, small tools, pencils, paintbrushes, and two boxes full of notebooks. We also have one more suitcase of civilian clothes and two cloth bags with a comforter waiting for us back in the storage warehouse. We will leave with more than twice the amount of stuff we arrived with. Somehow we managed to carefully pack our Angler-made mandolin into our Angler-made suitcase.

April 28, 1946

One more day left inside the barbed wire fences. I will be a free man tomorrow. No more dreary buildings. No more roll calls. No more bleached uniforms. I should be jumping for joy. Instead, I am filled with sadness. I am leaving the people whom I cherish and love, who have given me great support and friendship. Tomorrow I will enter a foreign world that I fear will be coldly different.

Perhaps there will be a day when I can be reunited with my good friends. I comforted myself by thinking that someday I might have a chance to meet up with the Okazaki-kun brothers and all the other men who have decided to remain in Canada.

I attended my last Judo Club meeting in the afternoon. I bid my club farewell. They thanked me for being a good friend and wished me well.

RELEASE FROM ANGLER

April 29, 1946

I awoke this morning feeling bewildered, like a bird in a familiar cage, afraid to fly from the door that had been left open. For four years we fought hard for justice, but no one heard our desperate cries. The Canadian politicians turned their heads away; the Japanese government was powerless to intervene. We had no place to turn in our small camp, only within ourselves. Upon awakening this morning, things looked better.

I looked at the foot of my bunk where my suitcases and bags were neatly piled. I made my bunk bed for the last time. I could not help but feel sadness over leaving this place, so indelibly attached had my life become to this camp. My heart ached as I glanced at my empty bookshelves. I felt a sudden and helpless contradiction, my mind yearns for a forgotten life of freedom and my heart is saddened by the loss of my accustomed surrounding.

I could hardly stomach breakfast this morning. I placed my half-eaten plate on the wash tray and went outside for a walk around the camp perimeter. I could see a group of internees awaiting to be released at the gate. I walked over and met my good friend Okazaki-kun. He was leaving this morning for southern Ontario. We have been so close over the past four years. He is a good friend and a fellow brother. Regardless of destiny and providence, I still felt it was unfair to part from my good friend. Okazaki-kun looked up and extended his hand for a farewell handshake. I took his hand in my own and felt a warm teardrop fall lightly upon my hand. My eyes began to swell with my own tears. He said, "Goodbye, good friend." My throat tightened and I could not speak. The wooden gate creaked open and Okazaki-kun left with the others. I saw him turn around a few times to glance back at the camp, and then he disappeared behind the hills. "*Sayonara*, goodbye my friend! Take good care of yourself. We might have a chance to meet again some day, as long as we remain in good health."

In the afternoon I made some last-minute preparations with my brother and my companions the Nishimura-kun brothers and Kitamura-kun, and at 4:00 PM our turn finally came to depart from Angler. At the front of the gate was a large group of internees waiting to give us their honoured farewell. I shook hands with the remaining Judo Club members. Many of them were in tears as they wished me good luck in my new life. The wooden gate began to open. Kawahira-kun came up to me and patted my shoulder with a big hand. In a trembling voice, he said, "*Ganbarun da zo*, don't give up! Take care of yourself!" I replied, "*Sayonara*, you will always be my good friend, Gune-chan."

The gate closed behind us with a heavy clanking sound. Our small group had made it outside. We had all passed through this gate so many times in the past four years, but this time we were certain to never return. *Sayonara* my loving friends. I must leave you behind. Goodbye to you, unweathered wire fence and faceless watchtowers. I inhaled deeply. Even though I have prepared myself in the last few weeks for this moment, always reminding myself that I would be free and responsible for my own livelihood, I still cannot shed the shadow of sadness and resentment that stains my character. I have spent my youth enclosed behind a barbed wire fence, banished from the society of men, punished for my wilful stand against my own native country.

I will never forget the countless experiences I have had during the four years of my internment. There were spirited moments when I shouted for what I truly believed was right. There were hearty moments of companionship with others who shared my fate. There were precarious moments that left me in a cold sweat for fear that I might be executed by a nervous guard.

These past four years have not been a total loss. I learned so many great things—judo, kendo, reading, writing, and so much more. Most important of all, I learned how to cope with hardships. I was fortunate to have been taught by great individuals who loved friendship and were patient in their instruction. I will always remember the sight of the solitary wild daisies in the sand. Tiny white flowers that bloomed so valiantly on the desolate soil beyond the high wire fences. The sight of them always brought me great hope, inspiring my despairing heart and leaving me with a fresh outlook.

Our group walked towards the storage warehouse. I glanced back with emotion to the camp I was leaving. It seemed faded to me, as though an old picture weathered by time. We entered the warehouse and were given our original suitcases and the cloth bags that had been confiscated from us. I removed my red-patched uniform and changed into my old and wrinkled civilian clothes. My suit felt damp and smelled musty. My suitcase had been piled among hundreds of other suitcases in a dark corner of the storage warehouse for more than four years.

It feels uncomfortable to be in civilian clothing. Shig remarked that our uniforms seem to have fit us much better. I had thought that once I was dressed in my suit, I would leap for joy and let out an excited hooray! But now I am stiff in my clothes. All I could do was sigh as I smoothed out the wrinkles in my suit and tried to shape my stretched-out hat. I brushed the dust from my brown shoes, almost new at the time I had handed them over to the guard four years ago. We re-packed our belongings and our group walked over to the army head-quarters to make the final claims for our departure. We received a train ticket for Winnipeg, Manitoba, and eleven dollars each for spending money. *Sayonara*, goodbye, Angler.

I shift aimlessly within the deserted station, waiting quietly for the train to arrive. It seems unusual that no guard is present. I watch as the train began to slow down on its approach. It arrived to take me to my new and uncertain future and I boarded the coach and sat down comfortably beside an open window. Looking outside, I saw the barren hills that had crested the place that had been my home for the last four years. I caught myself glancing back for an official or guard, but there was none. I remained seated beside my brother and fell asleep dreaming of what tomorrow would bring. Goodbye wild daisies.

POSTSCRIPT

I refer to Petawawa and Angler as concentration camps in my book to distinguish them from the internment camps for Japanese Canadians located in the interior of BC. The Japanese Canadians located at Petawawa and Angler were imprisoned in a maximum-security penitentiary. The compounds were surrounded by three layers of barbed wire fences and watchtowers. We were under the constant surveillance of rifle-ready military guards. We were not actually prisoners of war or even criminals. We were merely civilians who were declared dangerous individuals by the Canadian government.

In the beginning of May 1946, the Angler camp closed down and the remaining internees were relocated to Moose Jaw, Saskatchewan. They were confined to a minimum-security area until the time that they decided to be repatriated to Japan or to remain in Canada. All told, approximately four thousand Japanese Canadians were repatriated to Japan.

In September 1988 the Canadian government formally apologized to the Japanese Canadian people in the form of a Redress Agreement. Japanese Canadians affected by the Canadian government, either born or living in Canada between 1942 and 1949, were each compensated by payment of the sum of $21, 000. With my share of the money, I visited Japan in high style.

Japanese Canadians suffered greatly during the war. Yet, to this day, I am convinced that the end result was very much in the favour of the Japanese Canadians, especially for our Canadian *sansei* and *yonsei* generations.

I thank you for reading my story. I wanted to share with the good people around me a part of my life that changed me forever. I am happy with the decisions that I made and do not regret a single moment of my life.

Domo arigato,
Tom Sando Kuwabara

GLOSSARY

Aikoku Koshin Ky-oku — popular Japanese marching song
ashi-waza — judo foot tricks
baiu — rainy season
bento — lunch
do hyo ba — wrestling ring
do jo ba — judo hall
domo arigato — thank you very much
donguri — acorn
endo mame — green pea
ganbare — don't give up!
ganbari-ya — die-harder
ganbarun da zo — Let's not give up!
haiku — a seventeen-syllable verse Japanese poem
hi no maru — Japanese flag
issei — first generation of Japanese Canadians
judo-ba — judo hall
judo-gi — judo uniform
kagezen — a meal for an absent person
kansha — gratitude
kendo — Japanese fencing
Kimigayo — the Japanese national anthem
Kokyo no haha — a popular Japanese song

kotatsu — a foot warmer

kun — dear friend, Mr. (a salutation)

Meiji setsu — the Meiji Emperor's birthday

manju — bean jam on a bun

naniwa bushi — a storyteller

newaza — judo moves and holds in the laying position

nidan — judo black-belt holder

nigiri-meshi — rice ball

nisei — second generation of Japanese Canadians

nudo — a large Buddhist monk

-san — Mr. (a salutation)

sansei and yonsei — third and fourth generation Japanese
     Canadians

sayonara — goodbye

sensei — a teacher

sensu — a Japanese fan

shika ta ga nai — it cannot be helped (an expression)

shogi — a Japanese chess set

shoyu, miso — soy sauce, soybean soup

sora mame — straight bean

sora wa wakai — Japanese popular song

tachi waza — judo tricks in the standing position

toraware no mi — a prisoner

ukemi — technique of how to fall without injury

waza — judo tricks

ya demo teppo demo koi — I wasn't afraid of anything (an
     expression)

yohai — a salute

yonkyu — fourth grade in judo

ACKNOWLEDGEMENTS

A special word of thanks to my nieces Donna Donnelley and Viola Adams who helped me begin my project. I am very thankful to my daughter Annette and my close friend Elsa Polanka for giving me most needed encouragement. I thank NAJC for their support. My heartfelt thanks to Sherry Ishibashi for allowing me The Roar of the Great Lakes. I owe a special gratitude to my brother, Shig Kuwabara for his wonderful drawings. I give my sincere thanks to J.P. Desgagne for helping me complete *Wild Daisies in the Sand*.

Tom Sando was born in 1922 in northern British Columbia. After the death of his mother, he was sent to Japan to be raised and educated by his relatives, before returning to Canada at the age of sixteen. In 1942, Sando was imprisoned in Canadian concentration camps for being Japanese and for protesting Canada's unfair treatment of Japanese Canadians. After the war, Sando got a job in the construction industry, where he trained as a building foundation specialist in Winnipeg, Manitoba. He later moved to Edmonton, Alberta, where he worked for a large piling foundation company for thirty years, until he retired. Tom Sando currently lives in Edmonton, Alberta.